Cambridge Elements ≡

Elements in Cognitive Linguistics
edited by
Sarah Duffy
Northumbria University
Nick Riches
Newcastle University

SIGNED LANGUAGE AND COGNITIVE GRAMMAR

Sherman Wilcox
University of New Mexico

Rocío Martínez
University of Buenos Aires & National Scientific and Technical Council

Sara Siyavoshi
University of the Free State

CAMBRIDGE
UNIVERSITY PRESS

CAMBRIDGE
UNIVERSITY PRESS

Shaftesbury Road, Cambridge CB2 8EA, United Kingdom

One Liberty Plaza, 20th Floor, New York, NY 10006, USA

477 Williamstown Road, Port Melbourne, VIC 3207, Australia

314–321, 3rd Floor, Plot 3, Splendor Forum, Jasola District Centre, New Delhi – 110025, India

103 Penang Road, #05–06/07, Visioncrest Commercial, Singapore 238467

Cambridge University Press is part of Cambridge University Press & Assessment, a department of the University of Cambridge.

We share the University's mission to contribute to society through the pursuit of education, learning and research at the highest international levels of excellence.

www.cambridge.org
Information on this title: www.cambridge.org/9781009486842

DOI: 10.1017/9781108951326

First published 2024

A catalogue record for this publication is available from the British Library

ISBN 978-1-009-48684-2 Hardback
ISBN 978-1-108-94993-4 Paperback
ISSN 2633-3325 (online)
ISSN 2633-3317 (print)

Signed Language and Cognitive Grammar

Elements in Cognitive Linguistics

DOI: 10.1017/9781108951326
First published online: November 2024

Sherman Wilcox
University of New Mexico

Rocío Martínez
University of Buenos Aires & National Scientific and Technical Council

Sara Siyavoshi
University of the Free State

Author for correspondence: Sherman Wilcox, Wilcox@unm.edu

Abstract: This Element presents a Cognitive Grammar (CG) approach to a range of signed language grammatical phenomena. It begins with a background on the history of sign linguistics, focusing on what was a widely held belief that signs are simply gestures. The first section traces the modern linguistic examination of signed languages, focusing on Stokoe and his demonstration that these languages exhibit phonology and duality of patterning. Next, we present some fundamental principles that are foundational for cognitive linguistics and sign linguistics. In a section on Cognitive Grammar, we present a brief overview of CG principles, constructs, and models. Section 4 presents extensive analyses of signed language constructions applying CG, including nominal grounding; the concepts of Place and placing; a CG approach to "agreement" constructions in signed languages; reported dialogue; grammatical modality; and the grammatical meaning of facial displays. The final section examines the controversial role of gesture in grammatical constructions.

Keywords: signed languages, cognitive grammar, cognitive linguistics, gesture, grammatical constructions

ISBNs: 9781009486842 (HB), 9781108949934 (PB), 9781108951326 (OC)
ISSNs: 2633-3325 (online), 2633-3317 (print)

Contents

1 Elements of Sign Linguistics

1.1 What Are Signed Languages?

Signed languages are the natural languages used by communities of deaf people around the world. Although only scientifically studied since around the mid twentieth century, these signed languages have a long history of having been observed and written about. Deaf people and signed language were mentioned in ancient Egyptian writings from the nineteenth dynasty, c.1350–1200 BCE, where it was observed that deaf people "speak" with their hands. Signed languages are mentioned in Talmudic law, and in the writings of Aristotle and Quintilian. Writing about Roman oratorical gestures, Quintilian observed that movements of the hand and even a nod may express meaning; he believed that gestures such as this are used by deaf people as a substitute for speech.

  Throughout history, deaf people have gathered into groups in larger cities. We have a few historical descriptions of signed language communities, such as that of Pierre Desloges (1779 as reported in Lane & Grosjean 1980, pp. 123–124). Desloges became deaf at the age of seven from smallpox. As an adult, described the Parisian deaf community, noting that:

> There is no event in Paris, in France, and in the four corners of the world that is not a topic of our conversations. We express ourselves on all topics with as much orderliness, precision, and speed as if we enjoyed the faculties of speech and hearing.

The predominant historical view of signed languages has been that they are not language. Language, it was assumed, is spoken. Signs are produced with the hands, like gesture, and thus they were classified as *holistic gestures* – pantomimic images drawn with the hands lacking linguistic structure. One hundred years after Desloges wrote about the absolutely normal language abilities of deaf people, the view among those charged with educating deaf children was still that signs are merely gestures. In a speech to the Milan Conference of 1880 on the topic of methods for teaching deaf children, Giulio Tarra, the president of the conference, proclaimed (in Lane 1984, pp. 393–394):

> Gesture [i.e. sign] is not the true language of man which suits the dignity of his nature. Gesture, instead of addressing the mind, addresses the imagination and the senses. Moreover, it is not and never will be the language of society ... Thus, for us it is an absolute necessity to prohibit that language and to replace it with living speech, the only instrument of human thought.

Linguists now know a great deal about signed languages. We have learned about their grammatical structure; their geographic diversity and distribution; the presence of large communities of signed language users such as American Sign

Language (ASL), Argentine Sign Language (LSA), Brazilian Sign Language (Libras), Iranian Sign Language (ZEI), as well as much smaller communities of village languages such as San Juan Quiahije Chatino Sign Language (a village sign language used in the region of southern-central Oaxaca, Mexico), and Kata Kolok (a signed language used in a small traditional farming village in the north of Bali); and how these visually transmitted languages are perceived, acquired, and processed.

Sign linguists have demonstrated the many properties signed languages share with spoken languages, as well as some of the grammatical phenomena specific to signed languages that derive from their unique mode of production using visible hands, faces, and bodies – features such as constructed action (the use of the signer's body to depict the actions and movements of some person or entity), the semantic and phonological use of space, simultaneous constructions (the two hands producing different content), body partitioning (different parts of the body expressing different semantic content), and more.

1.2 Signed Languages Are Linguistically Structured

The view that signed languages lack linguistic structure can be expressed in the claim that they do not exhibit duality of patterning (Pulleyblank 1987; Pulleyblank 2011), the feature of language in which the meaningful elements, that is, words or morphemes, are composed of a small stock of meaningless elements, that is, sounds or phonemes (Hockett 1982). In other words, the claim was that signed languages have no phonology – the very name *phono*logy, after all, refers to "sound."

William C. Stokoe dispelled this view in his pioneering work *Sign Language Structure: An Outline of the Visual Communication Systems of the American Deaf* (Stokoe 2005)[1] by demonstrating that signs do have a level of sublexical structure equivalent to the phonemes of spoken words – that is, they exhibit phonology. Stokoe called these minimal elements cheremes, the root word *cher-* from Homeric Greek meaning "hand." He defined cheremes as "that set of positions, configurations, or motions which function identically [to phonemes] in the language" (Stokoe, 2005, p. 33).

Stokoe argued that the phonological units of signs fall into three major classes: *handshape* (the configuration that the hand makes when producing the sign), *location* (the place where the sign is produced, for example on the chest), and *movement* (the motion made by the signer in producing the sign, for example a path movement away from the signer's body). Stokoe called these

---

[1] We are citing the 2005 republication of Stokoe's original work, which appeared as Stokoe (1960), because it is currently the most accessible.

three *aspects* of a sign, observing that, unlike the sequential ordering of phonemes in spoken languages, cheremes occur simultaneously and cannot be produced independently: it is not possible to articulate a movement without also articulating a handshape to move or a place to make the articulation. Later these units came to be called sign parameters, and as more research was conducted, more parameters were identified. Battison (1978) recognized a fourth parameter, *orientation* (the direction the palm faces when a sign is produced). We will return to Stokoe's work and the topic of sign phonology in Section 7.1.

1.3 Signed Languages and Cognitive Linguistics

The field of sign linguistics has advanced enormously since the 1960s. Linguists working within different theoretical approaches and subfields of linguistics have contributed to our knowledge of the structure of the world's signed languages. An early and influential book on ASL linguistics, *The Signs of Language*, was published by Edward Klima and Ursula Bellugi and their colleagues (1979). Not long after, a series of influential books was published that ignited the field of cognitive linguistics, including George Lakoff and Mark Johnson's *Metaphor We Live By* (1980), Lakoff's *Women Fire and Dangerous Things* (1987), and Ron Langacker's *Foundations of Cognitive Grammar* (1987). Linguists soon began applying cognitive linguistic theory to the study of signed languages. Janzen and colleagues (2001, 2002, 2006, 2012) examined the linguistic use of space, the construal of events, and the cognitive factors at work in lexicalization and grammaticalization in signed languages. Working with Danish Sign Language, Engberg-Pedersen (1993, 1999, 2015) contributed to our understanding of the role of space and perspective. Shaffer (2002, 2004, 2016) applied force dynamics to the study of modality and advanced the study of evidentiality in ASL. Liddell (1995, 1998, 2000a, 2003) pioneered the application of conceptual blending theory to ASL. Expanding on this work, Dudis (2004) was the first to describe the conceptual underpinnings of body partitioning and investigated its role in conceptual blends.

Metaphor, metonymy, and iconicity have long been important domains of study in cognitive linguistics. These areas were recognized and studied by sign linguists working in other theoretical approaches (Brentari 2007; Emmorey 2014; Frishberg 1975; Wilbur 1987). Sign linguists working within cognitive linguistic theory have continued to explore these phenomena and their interactions in signed language lexicon and grammar across a number of languages (Emmorey 2014; Meir 2010; Nilsson 2016; Perniss 2007; Taub 2001; Wilcox 2000; Wilcox & Wilcox 2003; Wilcox et al. 2003).

1.4 Goals of This Element

We have three goals in writing this Element. We have for years worked within the theory of Cognitive Grammar. Although widely influential among spoken language cognitive linguists, Cognitive Grammar has not had a large impact within the field of sign linguistics. Thus, one of our goals is to provide sign linguists with the basic tenets of Cognitive Grammar and apply it to a range of signed language grammatical phenomena. Second, we hope to show readers with a background in cognitive linguistics and perhaps even Cognitive Grammar, but who have little or no experience with signed language data, examples of the kinds of unique phenomena sign linguists confront.

Our third goal addresses the question of how we approach the study of signed linguistics. Signed languages are languages with unique properties that set them apart from spoken languages. Since the beginning of their study within the modern science of linguistics, the modus operandi of the sign linguist has often been to take theories devised to account for spoken language structure, and search for analogies in signed languages. This was even the strategy first employed by Stokoe, who turned to the structuralist linguistics of the day to show that signs have the equivalent of phonemes and phonology. We believe it is time to adopt a new strategy, one which looks at signed languages with fresh eyes.

The great advantage of Cognitive Grammar, in our opinion, is that it provides a set of conceptual tools at an *appropriate* level of abstraction to implement this new strategy. We acknowledge, of course, that signed languages are human languages, and connections with spoken languages will surely be found – again, at the appropriate level of abstraction. Our cognitive linguistic perspective tells us to work with the assumption that these connections will reflect the conceptual abilities that all human share, abilities that are built up from our embodied sensorimotor experience with the world.

In the following sections we will provide a background on the concepts of Cognitive Grammar and its application to the analysis of various signed language phenomena. Before beginning that journey, Section 2 offers a proposal for how to approach the study of language, and especially of signed languages, from a cognitive perspective by reviewing what we know about embodied human perceptual and motor experience. Section 3 gives a background on key concepts of Cognitive Grammar, including the cognitive models that are pervasive in the theory.

Section 4 begins the application of Cognitive Grammar to signed language grammar. We introduce several new analytic concepts, drawn from Cognitive Grammar principles but unique to signed languages and the fact that they incorporate meaningful locations in space. We show its application to such grammatical phenomena as nominal grounding; antecedent-anaphor constructions; and referent tracking, including constructions that mark conceptual overlap. One example of conceptual overlap examined in detail is role shift, in which the signer can represent a narrator and various other characters in reported dialogue and narrative.

Section 5 offers a case study of grammatical modality, suggesting a possible source of modals in gesture. Data is drawn from Brazilian Sign Language, Italian Sign Language, and the depiction of gesture in Renaissance art. Section 6 looks at facial displays, relying on a Cognitive Grammar model called the control cycle and the concepts of effective control (striving to influence what happens in the world) and epistemic control (constructing and continually updating a conception of reality). The case is made that across many signed languages, effective control is often marked by a browed furrow facial display, and epistemic control is indicated by a mouth display made by depressing or pulling down the corners of the mouth. In Section 7 we return to Stokoe and examine the impact of his work not only on phonology but also on our understanding of certain grammatical constructions. One surprising new trend has been the re-emergence of gesture, with the claim that many sign constructions are fusions of language and gesture. We close this Element with a discussion of the relation between language and gesture informed by a cognitive linguistic perspective.

2 Fundamental Principles

In *Einstein's Unfinished Revolution*, physicist Lee Smolin describes his search for a way to make sense of the baffling theory of quantum physics and to unify the quantum with gravity. How, Smolin asks, do we start? "I have little idea how to search for scientific truth," he writes, "except by building on an existing research program, using a well-honed tool kit and methodology."

As sign linguists, we find that the best-honed tool kit and methodology is cognitive linguistics, specifically Cognitive Grammar. But even as well-developed as this theory is, when it comes time to apply it to signed languages new problems and possibilities emerge. In order to solve these problems and explore the possibilities we believe a preliminary step is necessary, and here Smolin offers guidance: "Start by writing down what you are confident we know for sure. Ask yourself which of the fundamental principles of the present canon must survive the coming revolution. That's the first page. Then turn again to a blank page and start thinking."

Before we turn the page to explore the elements of Cognitive Grammar and how it can be applied to the linguistic study of signed languages, we want to take Smolin's advice and write down some of the fundamental principles that underlie cognitive linguistics and Cognitive Grammar, as well as fundamental assumptions we make about how humans perceive, understand, and get along in the world.

Our only access to the world is through our senses. Perception is defined by the neuroscientist Gerald Edelman (1987, p. 26) as "the discrimination of an object or an event through one or more sensory modalities, separating them from the background or from other objects." Perception, he says, "involves categorization, a process by which an individual may treat nonidentical objects or events as equivalent." The problem then is one in which the animal must categorize and classify the things and events in its world. But an additional problem arises. The world does not provide a set of labels by which to classify the perceptual world. As Edelman (p. 32) observes, "there is no 'voice in the burning bush' telling the animal what the world description should be."

Edelman and numerous other cognitive scientists have developed a multitude of theories to account for how animals categorize their world, how they separate the foreground of perceptual focus from the background, and how they know when distinct perceptions are the same and when they are different. These theories all address the first fundamental principle:

> The world does not come to us labeled. The problem faced by any organism is to make sense of the world.

Making sense is understood here quite broadly. Again, according to Edelman, "whatever solutions to this problem are adopted by an individual organism, they must be framed within that organism's ecological niche and for its adaptive advantage" (p. 32). Making sense in this way can extend from a paramecium "figuring out" how to survive to a human child learning a particular system of grammatical expressions and how to use them.

All organisms are in this way meaning-making machines. If they don't make sense of the world, organisms die. Making sense is not an instructionist activity. The world does not inform an organism what is happening, how to act, what to do next, or how to survive. Making sense is more like a selectionist system. Like all selectionist systems it depends on the generation of a diverse population of variants and the selection of those which are most "adaptive" or successful. Making sense is selectionist in the sense that brains generate an ongoing population of concepts, ideas, guesses, propositions, and other cognitive creations which are matched to dynamically changing situations in the physical environment. Making sense is a dynamic, ongoing affair.

As we move to humans and human communication, we observe that while perception is the basis of embodied cognition, perception alone is not enough.

As Langacker (1979, p. 88) noted in an early exposition of Cognitive Grammar, "reality is not objectively given to us. Rather we structure reality in accordance with our own perceptual routines, cognitive abilities, expectations, beliefs, imagination, and desires." We structure reality: making sense of the world entails attributing meaning to objects and events. It is an active, constructive, and creative act.

The reality we are concerned with here is not physical reality but our conception of reality, especially as that conception is structured through language. Reality in this sense is ultimately a cultural construction. As the anthropologist Schneider (1976, p. 216) expressed it, "The world at large, nature, the facts of life, whatever they may be, are always part of man's perception of them as that perception is formulated through his culture. The world at large is not, indeed it cannot be, independent of the way in which his culture formulates his vision of what he is seeing .... Reality is itself constructed by the beliefs, understandings, and comprehensions entailed in cultural meanings." Making sense enables organisms to control their world. Cognitive Grammar describes this process as the control cycle (Langacker 2002): controlling or having an effect on the world, **effective control**, depends on making sense of the world, which is **epistemic control**. Organisms first must make sense of the world, so that they can control the world – or else the world will control them, usually leading to an unfortunate end.

For primates, including humans, arguably the most important perceptual system in terms of its impact on the evolution of cognition is vision. As neuroscientist Melvyn Goodale (1998, p. 21) wrote, "visual systems first evolved not to enable animals to see, but to provide distal sensory control of their movements. Vision as 'sight' is a relative newcomer to the evolutionary landscape, but its emergence has enabled animals to carry out complex cognitive operations on perceptual representations of the world." Indeed, describing vision in primates, the comparative anatomist Gordon Walls (1942) observed, "If asked what aspect of vision means the most to them, a watchmaker may answer 'acuity,' a night flier 'sensitivity', and an artist 'color.' But to animals which invented the vertebrate eye and hold the patents on most features of the human model, the visual registration of motion was of the greatest importance." Movement through space, encountering objects and entities in the physical spatial environment through visual and other perceptual abilities, not only allows us to make sense of our world, it drives the cognitive abilities that enable us to make sense. Perception and control of movement is a primary use of vision, and together they are deeply implicated in the development of an advanced cognitive system. Neuroscientist Rudolfo Llinás observes that "the evolutionary development of a nervous system is an exclusive property of actively moving creatures" (Llinás 2001, p. 17). As Chafe (1994, p. 53) has observed, consciousness is like vision:

> One way in which consciousness and vision are alike is in the very limited amount of information each can focus on at one time. There is foveal vision and focal consciousness. Surrounding this small area of maximum acuity lies, on the one hand, peripheral vision and, on the other hand, peripheral consciousness, both of which not only provide a context for the current focus but also suggest opportunities for its next moves. Beyond peripheral consciousness lies a vast treasury of information, some of which will at some time be brought into focal or peripheral consciousness, but all of which lies unattended at the moment. Consciousness and vision are alike in one other way as well. Both are in constant motion, the eye with its brief fixations, the mind with its continual shifting from one focus to the next. Both vision and consciousness exist in a state of constant restlessness.

In the development of an embodied theory of cognition and language based on perceptually grounded experience with the world, two fundamental principles emerge together:

> Vision is the primary sense of perception for primates, and the primary importance of vision is the perception of motion.

There is a hidden requirement here. Motion is a change in position or location over time. We do not, however, perceive motion as such, as some property of reality directly perceptible. We perceive *things that are in motion*.

Tying visual perception, as well as perception by other systems together with movement, we arrive at the next fundamental principle for the evolution of cognition:[2]

> Sensory-motor interaction with the world leads to embodied cognition: **No body, no brain.**

This principle is manifest in a basic assumption of cognitive linguists: "The kind of conceptual system we have is a product of the kind of being we are and the way we interact with our physical and cultural environment" (Lakoff & Johnson 1980, p. 119). Cognitive linguistics links embodied cognition to embodied language in the next fundamental principle:

---

[2] These assumptions are made in an evolutionary, not in an individual, sense. Under no circumstance are we implying that human individuals who have diverse experiences concerning their vision, their bodies, and their language(s) have "more or less body/vision," therefore "more or less brain/language," or any other ableist assumption.

> We must move our bodies to communicate. Language is embodied. **No body, no language**.

We mean this literally: humans communicate through the production of perceptible signals produced by articulatory movements of our bodies. In this sense, all language is embodied. All language is articulatory gesturing. As the cognitive scientist Ulrich Neisser (1967, pp. 156, 161) observed:

> To speak is to make finely controlled movements in certain parts of your body, with the result that information about these movements is broadcast to the environment. For this reason the movements of speech are sometimes called articulatory gestures. . . . There is every reason to believe that speech perception begins just as one aspect of the general perception of other people's movements.

Importantly, Lakoff and Johnson remind us of the cultural environment. Some view language as an essentially internal activity which only secondarily turns to external, interactive activity. A fundamental principle in our view is that language is first and foremost an interactive, social act. Thus language is dually grounded in embodied cognition and social interaction. Language is not only embodied, it is also embedded. Language at its heart serves and is defined by an interactive function.

> Social interaction and communication with others is fundamental to the organization of language. Language is socially embedded: **Nobody, no language**.

This fundamental principle is not shared by all linguists. Chomsky, for example, recently ruled out communication as a significant function of language:

> It has been, and still is, conventional to regard language as a system whose function is communication. To the extent that that characterization has any meaning, which is not very great, it appears to be incorrect actually in fundamental ways. The overwhelming use of language is internal, for thought. (reported in Fowler 2010, p. 1)

It seems to us that in many theories of language, production is assumed to have priority over comprehension. This view leads to the assumption that grammar is responsible for the generation of well-formed sentences. If making sense is a fundamental principle, this view is turned around: comprehension has priority over production. Production depends on comprehension, minimally because production requires that there are other beings who may understand what we have to say. While the most frequent use of language may be for internal thought, such internal communication surely develops first in interaction with others.

"Thinking," the linguist, psychologist, and Vygotsky scholar Vera John-Steiner, tells us, "is a soundless dialogue" (John-Steiner 1997, p. 210). "Language for the individual consciousness lies on the borderline between oneself and the other. . . . language is half someone else's" (Bakhtin 1981, p. 293). The conceit of the armchair linguist as philosopher is that internal thought precedes and does not require interacting with others.

A final fundamental principle pertains to communicative comprehension and production in interaction with others.

> Language is about making sense of our world, so that we can guide our interlocutors to make the same sense (or as close to the same sense as possible).

In other words, language is a basic means of achieving epistemic control and **intersubjective alignment** (Langacker 2017). Intersubjective alignment means simply that a particular linguistic expression is aimed at establishing momentary alignment in the interlocutors' scope of awareness and focus of attention. Scope of awareness and focus of attention pertains not only to conception but also to perception, and for signed languages, as we will see, this includes visual perception.

3 Elements of Cognitive Grammar

Before presenting some of the elements of Cognitive Grammar (CG), we offer the following caveats. The theory of Cognitive Grammar has a long history of development. Even before the publication of *Foundations of Cognitive Grammar: Theoretical Prerequisites* (Langacker 1987), Langacker was exploring this new approach in what he called **space grammar** in an early publication "Grammar as Image" (Langacker 1979). Aspects of Cognitive Grammar can also be seen in his work on functional stratigraphy (Langacker 1975). Langacker's own "basic introduction" to Cognitive Grammar runs to more than 500 pages (Langacker 2008), while his total output of books and articles on the theory runs in the hundreds – and that doesn't include the work of his students and others who adopt Cognitive Grammar as their theoretical framework. Our presentation can hardly scratch the surface of this comprehensive theory. Our presentation of elements of Cognitive Grammar is not intended to be exhaustive. We have selected aspects of the theory that are most relevant to the analyses of signed language phenomena presented in this Element.

Much of contemporary studies of signed languages assume a structuralist perspective, one in which language is built up from distinct and discrete building blocks such as phonemes or morphemes at various levels of structure:

lexicon, morphology, semantics, syntax, and so forth. CG claims instead that lexicon, morphology, syntax, and discourse "form a continuum of symbolic units that structure conceptual content for expressive purposes" (Langacker 1987, p. 35). Grammar consists solely in assemblies of symbolic structures – the pairing of a semantic structure and a phonological structure, such that one is able to evoke the other (Langacker 2008). Thus, symbolic structures are described as bipolar, consisting of a semantic pole and a phonological pole, often represented as S and P, respectively, in diagrams. Semantic structures are conceptualizations that signers and speakers recruit to express meanings. In CG, phonological structures are understood to include sounds, gestures, and orthographic representations. The essential feature of phonological structures is that they are able to be overtly manifested and perceived. Another way to think about phonological structures is that they are the result of bodily actions by a signer or speaker that produce some perceptible signal that is able to be perceived by a recipient. Any such perceptible signal is available to be interpreted as meaningful by a signer or a speaker and categorized as a linguistic symbol.

Semantic, phonological, and symbolic structures are not given a priori; rather, they emerge in use, and for this reason CG is considered a usage based approach. Language structure derives from usage events, instances of language use in discourse. Usage events may be of any size, complexity, and specificity. In terms of size, a usage event may consist of a word, a clause, a sentence, an intonation group, or an entire discourse. Complexity pertains to the semantic and phonological poles on their own, and to symbolic assemblies. Symbolic complexity is a defining property of human language – higher-level complex structures are formed out of lower-level simpler structures. A morpheme is definable in CG terms as an expression with zero symbolic complexity, or a degenerate symbolic assembly. Constructions are defined in CG in terms of symbolic complexity: a construction is "either an expression (of any size), or else a schema abstracted from expressions to capture their commonality (at any level of specificity)" (Langacker 2003, p. 43).

Specificity pertains to the degree or precision or detail of a structure. Specific structures are characterized with a high degree of detail or resolution; the converse of specificity is schematicity, a more coarse-grained characterization. This property falls along a continuum; for example, within the domain of nouns:

thing > creature > animal > bird > bluebird > Mountain Bluebird

Related to specificity and schematicity is the important concept of **schematization**, the process of extracting what is common across multiple experiences to arrive at a conception representing a higher level of abstraction (Langacker 2008, p. 17).

Schematicization is ubiquitous in language and language use. Schematicization is the process by which language structure is built up from usage events, the actual pronunciations and contextual understandings of linguistic units in a discourse. Specific forms are said to elaborate or instantiate more schematic structures. In the previous example, *bluebird* constitutes an elaboration or instantiation of *bird*.

Automatization is the process by which some complex structure becomes routinized, or entrenched so that is established as a unit. **Entrenchment** pertains at the level of the individual. Learning to ride a bicycle offers an example of entrenchment. When we first learn to ride a bicycle, we have to control a number of motor units: rotating the pedals, turning the handlebars, shifting our torso in order to maintain balance, and so forth. Turning a corner at first consists of controlling each of these elements individually, which usually results in falling over. Eventually, with practice, we acquire the skill to effortlessly and with little conscious monitoring turn a corner. We do so not by controlling each structural unit required to make a left turn, but simply by automatically executing the entrenched higher-order unit "left turn." In the same way, the motor activity of controlling the individual articles in producing a sign, or fingerspelling a name, involves controlling many elements. At first, learners of a signed language attempt to control each articulator individually. With practice, the many degrees of freedom are reduced. The individual articulators required to produce the fingerspelled letter F (in ASL, extending middle, ring, and pinkie finger, flexing the index finger and touching it near the tip with the thumb to produce a ring-shape, orienting the hand outward) are controlled as a single, entrenched unit: F. Entrenchment continues "upward" to form larger units consisting of more articulators, such as when the letters F and I, as in fingerspelling F-I-S-H, become entrenched as the unit FI.

Finally, symbolic structures of all types may also vary along the dimension of conventionality. **Conventionality** pertains at the level of the group. In CG, conventionality means simply that something is shared and known to be shared. Like entrenchment, conventionality is a matter of degree. A linguistic unit such as a word or expression may be shared by the majority of a language community or only by a small group of people – a village or even a household. Even within a community with shared conventional linguistic structures, no two individuals share exactly the same repertoire. In this sense, we all have different grammars.

Symbolic assemblies in turn vary along these parameters. Full-fledged expressions are phonologically specific; semantically, actually manifest expressions also tend to be more specific. Expressions that have attained both a level of entrenchment and conventionalization are regarded as lexical items. Linguistic structures that have not are novel expressions. Given the gradient nature of entrenchment and conventionalization, the boundary between the two is fuzzy and dynamic, indicated by the dashed line in Figure 1.[3]

The lexicon and grammar also consist of symbolic assemblies which vary along the parameters of schematicity and complexity, as shown in Figure 2.[4]

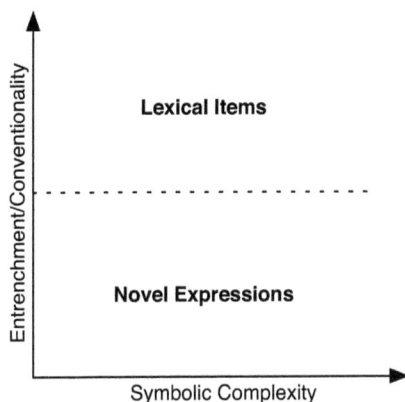

Figure 1 Lexicon and novel expressions
(Langacker, 2008 © Oxford University Press)

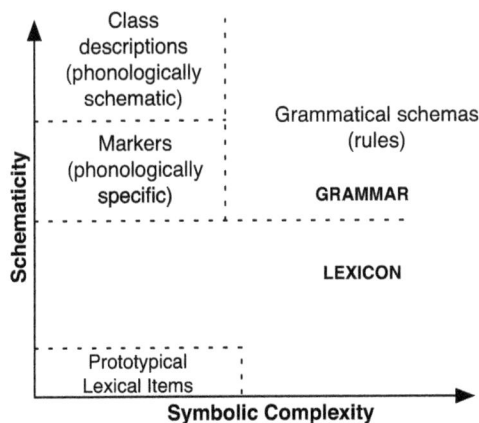

Figure 2 Symbolic complexity
(Langacker 2008 © Oxford University Press)

---

[3] Figure 1 conflates entrenchment (pertaining to a particular speaker) and conventionality (pertaining to a speech community).

[4] Figures 1 and 2 are based on Langacker (2008, p. 21).

Prototypical lexical items tend to be specific and symbolically less complex. However, the CG view adopts a broad view of lexical items. For signed languages, we will suggest that many elements that have been considered symbolically simple "signs" are often quite symbolically complex. Often, this symbolic complexity hides in highly schematic symbolic components, which are often simultaneously expressed.

Grammatical markers tend to be phonologically specific and capable of being expressed, but semantically quite schematic. Grammatical classes are defined in symbolic terms in CG; that is, grammatical classes such as noun, verb, or adverb are bipolar, having a schematic semantic pole and a schematic phonological pole. Thus, in CG we talk of a noun schema or a verb schema. As we will see, CG claims that these schemas are derived from experientially grounded conceptual archetypes.

Linguists approaching CG for the first time often ask, "where are the rules?" Rules are nothing more than schemas that form patterns by which a language user creates symbolically complex expressions: "Complex expressions consist of specific symbolic assemblies, and the rules describing them are schematic assemblies that embody their common features" (Langacker 2008, pp. 23–24). Thus, the grammar of a language consists of *structured inventory of conventional linguistic units* (Langacker 1987). In the CG view, grammar does not generate well-formed structures; rather, signers and speakers use their knowledge of this vast inventory of conventional linguistic structures, along with their general cognitive abilities, to create expressions. This applies at the level of morpheme or word (sign), as well as to syntax and discourse.

CG makes an important distinction between **autonomous** and **dependent** linguistic elements. A dependent structure is "one that is characterized to a significant degree in relation to another and consequently makes salient internal reference (at least in schematic terms) to a structure of the requisite type" (Langacker 1987, p. 300). A dependent structure makes reference to an autonomous structure, which functions to elaborate the dependent structure. This is called A/D asymmetry, and the principle applies to semantic and phonological structures. Phonologically, prototypical vowels are autonomous, while consonants are dependent, acting to change the more stable sonority of the vowel. Conceptually, relationships such as a spatial relation are dependent on their participants: "we cannot conceptualize a spatial relation (like *on*, *under*, or *near*) without to some extent (if only schematically) invoking the entities that participate in it" (Langacker 2008, p. 200). For signed languages, movement and spatial location are dependent: we cannot conceptualize a movement or a spatial location without schematically invoking some autonomous *thing* that moves or is located.

Baseline and **elaboration** organization is another significant property of language (Langacker 2016a). A baseline notion or structure is generally more substantive, more stable, already under control, or has some priority; elaboration consists of an operation, or a function that maps the baseline onto a higher-level baseline-elaboration (BE) structure. Elaboration may function to change or augment a baseline element; conceptual elaboration requires additional cognitive resources.

Baseline and elaboration subsumes autonomy and dependence. As we have seen, an autonomous structure may appear independently, while a dependent structure makes schematic reference to and requires an autonomous element for its full manifestation. Autonomous elements are thus more substantive and in some sense "prior" to dependent elements. Continuing the phonological example, Langacker suggests that prosodic stress is dependent on the sonority of a vowel, and thus describes it as an elaboration, an operation on the vowel which is the prior baseline element. Morphologically, stems are described as the baseline, which are elaborated by dependent affixes. Alternatively, we can say that affixes make schematic internal reference to an autonomous structure, the stem. As we just saw, movement is dependent, requiring an autonomous entity that moves; the baseline-elaboration description would say that the entity is the more substantive baseline structure, and movement is an operation that changes or elaborates the entity (e.g., it changes entity's spatial location).

One subtle, but significant, fact that emerges from this account pertains to compositionality. In many cases, combining elements may exhibit little A/D asymmetry, such as the compound *dog house*. In these cases, the components are equally substantive conceptually and phonologically, and may be said to constitute dual baselines (Langacker 2016a). However, when A/D asymmetry is most distinct, the dependent structure has no substance and is best described as an operation on an autonomous structure. Such is the case for prosodic stress, or a physical entity (autonomous, baseline structure) that is moving (nonsubstantive operation on the entity).

A final ubiquitous and significant aspect of language is the notion of the **ground** and **grounding** (Langacker 1987). The ground pertains to the communicative (speech and sign) event participants, their interaction, and the time and place of the communicative event. Words that explicitly refer to the ground include *I/me, you, here, there,* and *now*. **Grounding elements** specify the relation between the ground and nominal or clausal expressions. Nominal grounding directs the interlocutor's attention to an intended discourse referent. Grounding elements that pertain to nominal grounding include demonstratives (*this, that, those, a, the,* etc.). Clausal grounding pertains whether an event actually does occur – that is, to a signer's or a speaker's conception of reality (see *reality model* in the following section). Thus, grounding indicates the epistemic status of profiled elements – things or processes – in relation to the interlocutors.

Profile is a central concept in Cognitive Grammar. The profile is the focus of attention within the immediate scope of an expression. The profile is what the expression designates or refers to. While grounding elements direct attention to and profile a thing or an occurrence, an essential feature of grounding elements is that the ground itself remains offstage and unprofiled. For example, in nominal grounding, although the *this/that* distinction expresses distance from the speaker (often in an abstract domain), the speaker as ground remains offstage and unprofiled in an expression such as *that cat over there*. The same is true for clausal grounding. Examples of clausal grounding include tense markers and modals (Langacker 2008; Langacker 2019). The past tense marker *-ed* evokes the time of speaking, which is an aspect of the ground, but it does not profile the time of speaking as would, for example, *now*. Semantically, grounding elements are characterized by quite schematic meaning. As a result, grounding elements lie toward the more grammatical end of the lexical/grammatical continuum shown in Figure 2, with meanings that construe elements rather than express specific lexical content (Langacker 2008).

3.1 Interlude: Space, Time, and Language

Language both occurs in space and time and represents space and time. As a physical activity, language takes place in space and time at several different levels of organization. At the contextual level, the speaker is situated spatially and temporally when she speaks. The act of signing or of speaking involves the movement through space and time of articulators. The neural activity which underlies speaking and signing also has a spatial and temporal dimension. Language also represents space and time: we use language to talk about objects and events which exist in space and time. Even when we talk about concepts that have no referents in the physical world, we typically conceptualize these metaphorically as objects or events (Lakoff 1987; Lakoff & Johnson 1980; Lakoff & Johnson 1999; Johnson 1987). As we will see in more detail, it is even possible to characterize two of the basic grammatical elements of language, nouns, and verbs, as abstract schemas of space and time.

Space, time, matter, and motion are essential elements of our perceptually and experientially grounded world. Objects are located in space and time, and they move through space and time. Events and actions, although they depend on things such as people, trees, animals, and other material entities, consist of a change that unfolds through time.[5] In cognitive approaches such as Cognitive Grammar, the claim is that our perceptually grounded experience of the world has direct significance for grammar.

The dimensions of space and time in which language is realized have differing roles within linguistic representation. At the contextual level, for example, space and time are important aspects of language because they form the ground for the communicative act. The speaker's or signer's location in space finds linguistic expression as a part of the ground (*here, there, behind*, etc.), as does the speaker's location in time (*now, yesterday, tomorrow*).

Space and time have special significance for signed languages. Not only are lexical signs produced in space; space plays a ubiquitous role in expressing grammatical relations and constructions. We will see in Section 7 that the linguistic status of locations in space is currently highly controversial. Just as for spoken languages, signed languages are expressed in time. While spoken languages often metaphorically express time in terms of space (e.g., *what are the events that are ahead of us?* or *That was way back in 1900*), signed languages express time literally in space (Engberg-Pedersen 1999; Fischer & Gough 1978; Frishberg & Gough 2000; Pereiro & Soneira 2004; Stokoe et al. 1965).

3.2 The Experiential Grounding of Language and Grammar

The view that we present is one of language and grammar as grounded in experience, embodied in perception and action; that is, it is *built-up* from experience rather than *built-in* as an innate cognitive module or self-contained ability. The perceptual events at which our embodied experience is directed consist of objects and events in the world. Things such as rocks, trees, animals, and other people are located in places; they move about (rocks roll, trees sway); they perform actions on other things (rocks tumble down hills and knock down trees). As we have noted, our fundamental drive is to make sense of this perceptual world. We try to figure out what these things are, where they are located, how they move about, what they are doing.

These are the perceptible elements in the world from which conceptual archetypes emerge. Conceptual archetypes are pervasive and experientially grounded "complex notions, intermediate in their level of abstraction, that pertain to fundamental aspects of moment-to-moment experience" (Langacker 2014, p. 31). A partial list of conceptual archetypes includes: a physical object, an object in a location, an object moving through space, the human body, the

---

[5] The perception of time is, of course, an enormously complex and much-debated topic, incorporating the question of whether time even exists (Rovelli 2014).

human face, a whole and its parts, a physical container and its contents, seeing something, holding something, handing something to someone, exerting force to effect a desired change, a face-to-face social encounter (Langacker 2008). Conceptual archetypes may be manifest in the mental domain, such as the experience of perceiving, of thinking, and of feeling emotions, or in the physical domain as a type of "force-dynamic" experience: muscular exertion, being subjected to forces, resisting and overcoming forces, or carrying out a physical action (Langacker 2000). Although the term focuses on their role in conception, conceptual archetypes consist of meanings and perceptible forms. They always come to the perceiver as a pairing of a perceptible form, and some basic meaning: this is a person, that is a tree; that person located far from me; the rock is located near to me; the animal is moving toward me. Conceptual archetypes are forms with meaning: they are archetypal symbolic structures.

Grammatical structure is grounded in conceptual archetypes. For example, one conceptual archetype involves a global setting in which mobile participants appear in certain locations, and then interact in some event in which energy is transferred from one participant to the other. This conceptual archetype forms the experiential basis of clause structure, including archetypal grammatical roles such as agent and patient, a transitive verb, and so forth.

We can think of conceptual archetypes in terms of baseline and elaboration. A baseline structure is more substantive and has some priority. A physical object in a location is a baseline conceptual archetype. An object moving through space is one type of elaboration. Further elaborations result in the global setting archetype with participants (things) in locations interacting and transferring energy.

This analysis also applies to sign phonology. Hands are substantive things with certain properties, or aspects: the hand's configuration, location, and orientation. Elaborations can operate on each of these properties. Bending or fluttering the fingers is an elaboration of handshape, as is changing the hand's orientation. Movement can elaborate the hand's location. As we've seen, elaborations can operate on BE structures. An example of such a higher level elaboration is manner of movement, which elaborates movement, which in turn elaborates location. This analysis also suggests that the basic phonological elements of signed languages are conceptual archetypes: hand (object), location (object in a location), and movement (object moving through space). This approach accommodates facial articulators as well. The human face is a baseline element (Langacker 2008). Elaborations are often expressed as verbs operating on a baseline structure: we *stress* a syllable, *accent* a vowel. Expressing facial displays as elaborations of baseline facial structures, we *furrow* the brow, *squint* the eyes, *pull the corners of the lips down*, *nod* or *shake* the head, *look up, look down* with the eyes, and so forth. These are only simple examples, leaving a great deal of detail and complexity to be explored and explained. We believe, however, they demonstrate how CG principles can be applied not just to semantic structure but also to phonological structure.

We have mentioned that grammatical classes are defined in symbolic terms in CG. Conceptual archetypes play a central role here. We have seen that two basic conceptual archetypes are a physical object, and energetic interactions or events. Langacker (2008, p. 104) describes how these form the basis at the prototype level of noun and verb grammatical categories. For nouns:

1. A physical object is composed of material substance.
2. We think of an object as residing primarily in space, where it is bounded and has its own location.
3. In time, on the other hand, an object may persist indefinitely, and it is not thought of as having any particular location in this domain.
4. An object is **conceptually autonomous**, in the sense that we can conceptualize it independently of its participation in any event.

For verbs:

1. An energetic interaction is not itself material, consisting instead of change and the transfer of energy.
2. Thus an event resides primarily in time; it is temporally bounded and has its own location in time.
3. By contrast, an event's location in space is more diffuse and also derivative, as it depends on the locations of its participants.
4. This is so because an event is **conceptually dependent**; it cannot be conceptualized without conceptualizing the participants who interact to constitute it.

We emphasize that experientially grounded archetypes account for the prototype characterizations of nouns and verbs. Characterizations that are valid for all instances must occur at the schematic level. Certain general cognitive abilities are recruited to arrive at these schemas. For nouns, the schematic characterization is called a **thing** (used in a specific technical sense), which is the result of grouping and reification (reification allows us to conceptually manipulate a group of entities as a unitary higher-order structure). For verbs, the schematic characterization relies on two cognitive abilities: the capacity for apprehending relationships and the ability to track relationships through time (Langacker 2008, p. 108).

We have seen that many of the properties of language, such as autonomy-dependence, schematicity, and complexity apply to the semantic pole and the phonological pole of symbolic structures. The same is true for conceptual archetypes, which emerge from our embodied physical interactions with the world, including the social world of interacting with others. By saying that they are embodied, we mean that these conceptual archetypes are built up from perceptual and motor interactions with physical objects in the world. We see objects moving, changing their locations, and interacting energetically. Thus, while these experiences give rise to conceptualizations, they are grounded in physical perceptual abilities (hearing, vision, touch, etc.) and in physical motor abilities. This is, in a very general sense, the phonological level – the level at which we produce the physical actions that result in signals perceptible by others.

We emphasize this view because it is this embodied, perceptual, motoric, physical level in which *signed language phonology occurs*: things acting, hands changing shapes, hands moving and changing locations. In a very real sense, the raw material of sign phonology is one of the experiential sources of conceptual archetypes; or, to put it the other way around, sign phonology is an *expressive* manifestation of *conceptual* archetypes.

3.3 Cognitive Models

Cognitive grammar relies on several cognitive models incorporating and building on conceptual archetypes to account for various aspects of language and grammar. We will describe some of these conceptual archetypes and cognitive models in more detail in later sections as we show how they apply to the analysis of signed languages. Here, we briefly describe a few of the cognitive models used in the analysis of grammar.

1. **Stage Model**: a cognitive model which characterizes a fundamental aspect of our perceptual experience: observing external events which involve the interaction of participants within a setting (Langacker 1991b, p. 284). The stage model evokes the visual experience of watching a play take place on a stage. The maximal scope of our visual attention includes the entire stage; viewers focus their limited visual attention on the actors who occupy locations on stage and interact with each other. The viewers in the audience remain off-stage. As the central action onstage, the participants and their interaction define the immediate scope. Within the area onstage, attention is directed at a particular element, called the profile.

2. **Billiard Ball Model**: closely related to the stage model and the global setting conceptual archetype is a model in which discrete objects move through space and interact energetically. Their motion may be driven by some external force, or by some internal force; in either case, energy is transferred by forceful

physical contact from the moving object to the impacted object (Langacker 1991b). This model is the basis for a conceptual account of clause structure.

3. **Canonical Event Model**: this cognitive model (Figure 3) combines elements of the stage model and the billiard ball model. The cognitive event model combines the viewing arrangement of the stage model with a viewer observing the onstage action, with the conception of these onstage participants interacting and transmitting energy (Langacker 1991b).

4. **Reality Model**: a model which the world unfolds in a certain way out of all the conceivable ways. Reality is the history of occurrences. As this is a conceptual model, each person has his or her own conception of reality. The reality model plays a significant role in a cognitive account of modals (Langacker 2013).

5. **Control Cycle**: the control cycle describes a ubiquitous phenomenon consisting of four phases. The control cycle may be manifest in several domains, including physical, mental, perceptual, and linguistic. The best way to understand the control cycle is with a simple physical example: a frog catching a fly. In the first phase, the frog is at rest; this is the baseline phase, and the frog is an **actor**, having various aspects of its life under control. This is called the frog's **dominion**. In the second, some **target**, in this case the fly, enters the frog's field (in this example, the frog's perceptual field), resulting in a state of tension. In the third phase, the frog undertakes some **action**: it catches and ingests the fly. As a result, the frog is once again

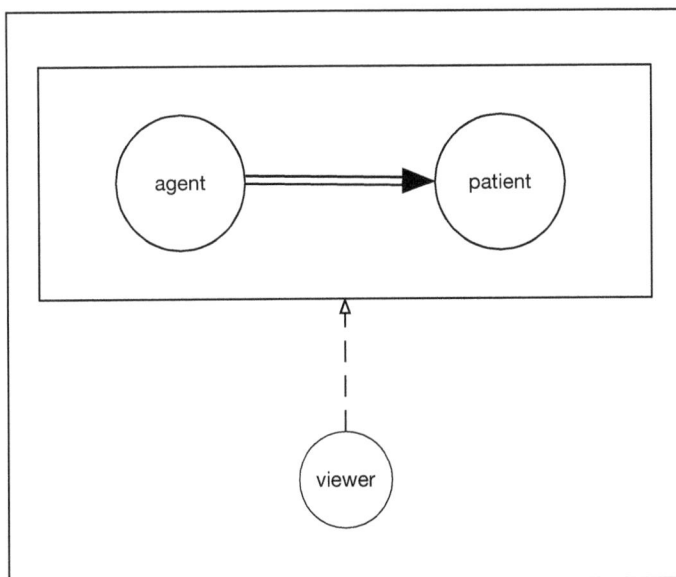

Figure 3 Canonical event model

in a period of stasis or rest in the fourth phase. The control cycle is manifest in two ways. We have already introduced the first way in the fundamental principle of *making sense* or **epistemic control**, which pertains to our knowledge of the world. The second way that the control cycle is manifest is in **effective control** – our effort to have some effect on or to influence the world. Of course, humans are entities in the world. Effective control is not only the effort to influence others, but ourselves, and so effective control extends to mentally or physically adapting to the world. The control cycle is manifest in several ways in language, including the grammatical expression of possession, modality (both root and epistemic), the expression of assertions, and so forth. We will apply the control cycle to the analysis of facial displays in signed languages in Section 6.

6. **Reference Points**: reference points are a general cognitive ability that are manifest in all aspects of our experience. Reference points "invoke the conception of one entity for purposes of establishing mental contact with another" (Langacker 1993, p. 5). For example, if we wish to direct someone's attention to a location we might say, "Do you know where the university library is? Well, the linguistics department is directly across from there." The library serves as a reference point for mentally locating the desired target of attention, the linguistics department. Reference points appear in possessives, topic constructions, relative clauses, antecedent-anaphor relations, metonymy, and in our analysis of pointing constructions in Section 4.1.

4 Signed Language and Cognitive Grammar

Two core imperatives of being alive and staying alive are making sense of the world and controlling the world. These two imperatives are manifestations of a ubiquitous aspect of experience, the control cycle (Langacker, 2002). Making sense of the world requires epistemic control by constructing and continually updating a conception of reality: what are the objects that populate our experiential world, did an event occur, is it likely to occur? Effective control describes our striving to influence what happens in the world. The two are interrelated because in order to influence what happens in the world, we must have some basic understanding of it.

In the domain of language, these imperatives are manifest at many levels. When we communicate we are trying to achieve effective control by influencing our interlocutor in order to achieve intersubjective alignment: we want our interlocutor to have in mind the same thing we have in mind in a given discourse context, to see things the way we see them. At its most basic level, our interlocutor has to be able to identify the objects we are conceptualizing out of the vast universe of conceivable entities. This is described in CG as identification, and it is achieved by **nominal grounding** – relating the conceived object to the ground. Making sense and achieving epistemic control also must include knowledge of occurrences and their status in relation to reality; this aspect of epistemic control pertains to clausal grounding. We address nominal grounding next. Clausal grounding is taken up in Section 5.

4.1 Nominal Grounding

Nominal grounding may be understood as a kind of conceptual pointing: the signer or speaker uses various linguistic resources such as demonstratives to conceptually direct the interlocutor's attention to – point to – the intended referent. Langacker (2016b) considers pointing to be a kind of linguistic symbol and suggests that an act of pointing is a good point of departure for understanding definite nominal grounding, observing that "a demonstrative constitutes a kind of mental pointing (often accompanied by a physical pointing gesture)" (Langacker 2009, p. 121). Figure 4, from Langacker (2016b), depicts the CG characterization of a prototypical act of pointing.

In the diagram, G is the actual ground in the current speech event. S and H are the speaker and hearer, where these terms are extended to mean the interlocutors producing (S) and perceiving (H) the pointing. The current discourse environment (or discourse space, CDS) includes the visually accessible immediate physical context. This onstage (OS) region contains a number of things (the circles) which could be singled out by pointing. The solid arrow represents the pointing finger directed at FOC, the focus of attention. The act of pointing has directive force (the double arrow), instructing the addressee to follow, both visually and conceptually, its direction. As a result both interlocutors focus their

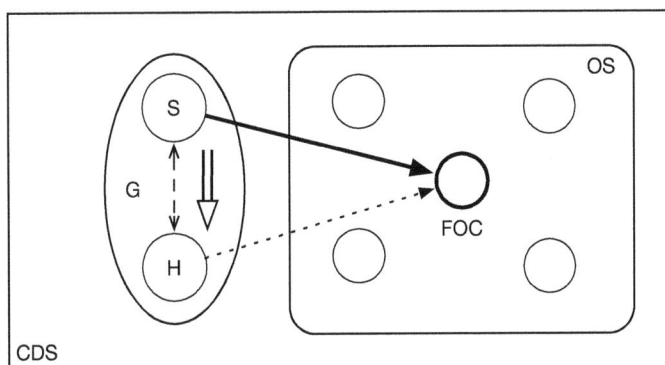

Figure 4 Pointing in cognitive grammar
(Langacker, 2016b, used with permission)

attention on the same entity, the intended referent. The focused referent is shown in bold to indicate that it is the entity that is profiled.

Pointing Is a Construction

We have seen that conceptual archetypes may range from simple concepts such as a physical object to more complex scenes such as the global setting archetype. Pointing is a complex conceptual archetype composed of component elements. The seventh-century Chinese Buddhist monk Huineng observed that "when the wise man points at the moon, the fool looks at the finger." We see here the two components of pointing: the moon, which is the focus of attention, and the finger, which directs attention to the moon but is not (except for fools) the focus of attention.

These two components of pointing have been made explicit in a cognitive linguistic account of pointing (Martínez & Wilcox 2019; Wilcox & Occhino 2016). This analysis reveals that pointing is a construction consisting of two component symbolic structures – the device or means of directing attention, which carries with it directive force, and the focus of attention. These two components are termed a **pointing device** and a **Place**,[6] each consisting of a form and a meaning. Figure 5 depicts the two component symbolic structures and the (bolded) composite pointing construction. Ellipses in the phonological pole of the pointing device indicate schematicity, subsuming, for example, index finger, hand, eye gaze, body orientation, or even a pointing instrument such as a pencil. The only phonological specification of the pointing device is that it has to be capable of directing attention by pointing. The pointing device and its directive force instruct

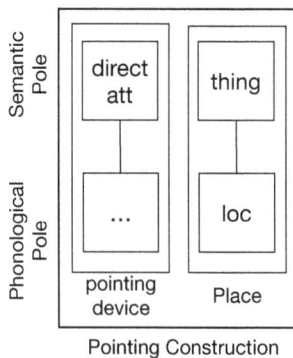

Figure 5 Pointing construction

---

[6] Place is capitalized to signify that it is the name of the entire symbolic structure; the phonological pole is called the location.

the addressee to follow its direction, so that both participants in the communicative event focus their conceptual attention on the same entity, the semantic pole of the Place symbolic structure. The only specification of phonological pole of Place is a spatial location (LOC). The schematic semantic pole of Place is "thing" – something conceived as a single entity.

Places arise through the process of schematization acting on our perceptual and experiential world. Consider the experience of two friends having cappuccinos in their favorite coffee shop. One person points to the coffee cup and says, "Look at this cup. Isn't it cute?" In pointing, he directs attention to an object in a location, the experiential archetype for a Place. We can extend this account to encompass many different situations. We point to objects that are present (and known to be present) in the physical environment but not visible, such as a familiar building that is too far away or blocked by other buildings to be seen, or a distant mountain the view of which is blocked by trees. We may point to a location that was formerly occupied by some object that has not been present in that location for years, decades, or even centuries. For example, upon visiting a childhood home with a friend, one might say, "This [pointing to a location in the living room] is where my piano was when I was a child." In signed languages, as we will see, we can point to entities that exist but are not and never were in the current spatial environment, a type of anaphoric reference. We can also point to virtual or abstract entities, such as ideas, schools of thought, emotions, and so forth. This latter use of Places is especially productive in contrastive constructions (Winston 1995).

As a signer perceives and produces more of these usage events, she abstracts away from the semantic and spatial specifics of any particular entity and its location, extracting what is common across multiple experiences to arrive at a schematic Place symbolic structure. Schematization operates at both poles of the symbolic structure – semantic and phonological. The spatial location of an entity is, for signed languages, an aspect of its phonology. The location of the signer's nose, eyes, and ears is irrefutably specified phonologically. By extension, the spatial location of the cappuccino cup, a mountain, and even the remembered piano is for a signer a phonological location.

Thus, Places are abstracted from actual usage events – in this case, the archetypal usage event of pointing to a physical object in a spatial location. Being schematic, a Place has neither a specific meaning nor a specific spatial location; rather, Places are symbolic structures that associate a schematic meaning with a schematic phonological (spatial) location. In a usage event, the schematic meaning and the schematic location are instantiated, resulting in a fully contextualized Place. In a usage event, a signer directs attention to the phonological pole of the Place, its location, and because of the association between the phonological pole and the semantic pole of symbolic structures, the signer thereby directs attention to the intended referent.

An important aspect of schematic meanings is that they are **immanent** in their instantiations. Immanent meanings 'lie within' those of instantiating expressions, which elaborate them ('flesh them out') in their own individual ways" (Langacker 2009, p. 14). The more schematic concept of *liquid* is immanent within the specific instance *water* and *cappuccino*. Immanence is a central notion in CG present in a host of expressions, including possessives, reference point phenomena, epistemic versus root modality, and grammatical categories. Immanence also pertains to cognitive abilities. Conceiving an object moving through space requires mental scanning through time in the spatial domain. Langacker (1993, p. 4) points out that we are usually not aware of the mental scanning as a separate mental experience "precisely because it is immanent in (or manifested through) the richer, more contentful conception of spatial motion by a physical object." Just as mental scanning is immanent in the conception of an object moving through space, schematic Places are immanent within the objects with which they spatially coincide.

Because of the range of entities that we point to – physically and visually present cups, missing cups, unseen but still physically existing buildings, the memory of the location of a childhood piano, and more – we can posit a continuum of Places (Figure 6).

Points along the continuum can be described with respect to various dimensions. One dimension is spatial, temporal, and conceptual immediacy. Spatially present objects fall at the left end of the continuum; they are real, and visual perception provides direct access to the physical entity and its Place. Temporal immediacy pertains to the present moment. Temporally distant, nonimmediate, experiences require progressively greater conceptual resources. Experiences such as the missing cappuccino cup require recall: one must know and remember that the cup was present in the current discourse environment. The cognitive load here is fairly minimal. The same is true to an extent for the building or mountain that cannot be seen: visual perception is no longer available, requiring memory and a mental projection that the entity is still in existence. Naturally time is a factor as well: the longer the time between present and when the cup, the mountain, or the building was seen requires great memory. The childhood piano falls farther along the continuum. Pointing to the location occupied by the childhood piano places an even greater load on memory and mental projection. At the far right are virtual and imaginary entities (e.g., theories) and real but nonpresent entities which exist independently of any particular spatial location, but are used in anaphoric pointing constructions. These and other factors determine in a complex interaction the cognitive resources required.

From the viewpoint of how humans perceive and construct concepts of our experiential world, locations do not exist. We see objects that occupy locations.

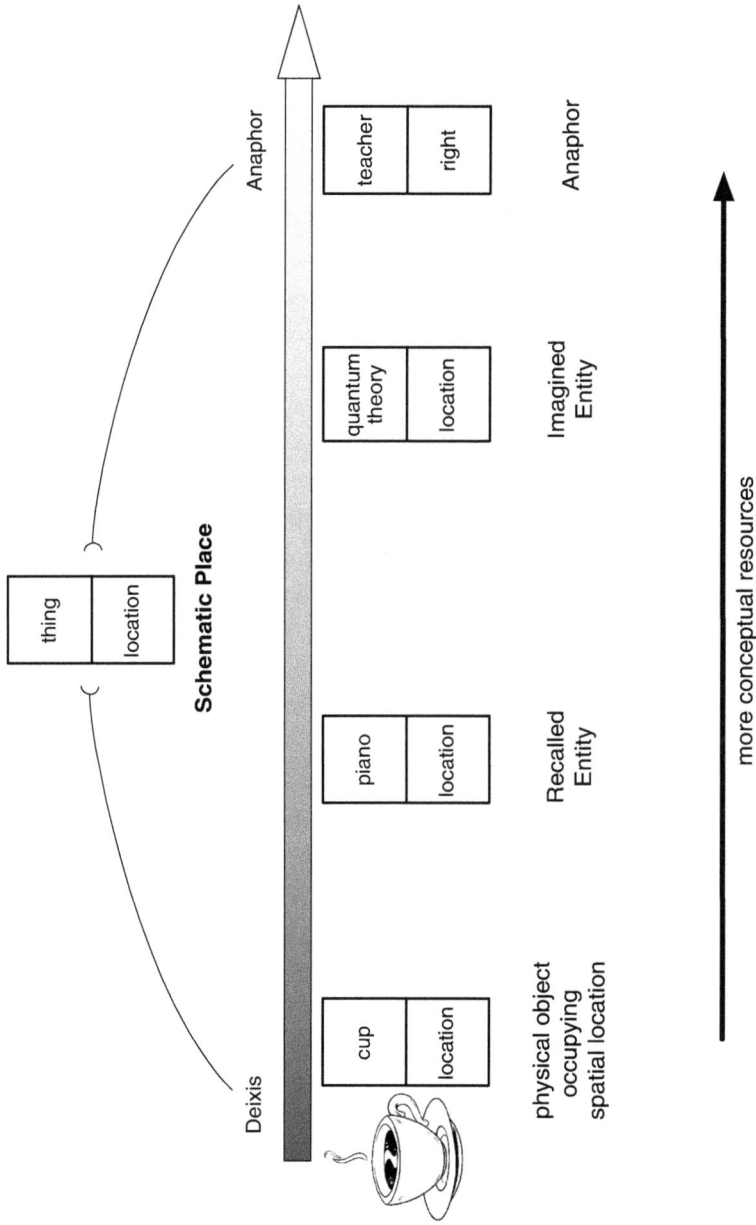

Schematic Place

Deixis · Anaphor

thing
location

cup		piano		quantum theory		teacher
location		location		location		right

physical object occupying spatial location · Recalled Entity · Imagined Entity · Anaphor

more conceptual resources

Figure 6 Places continuum

This is the experiential basis of the conceptual archetype *object in a location*. This is also the perceptual and experiential basis of Places. The baseline Place, perceptually and developmentally, is a perceptible, physical object. With elaboration requiring increasing cognitive resources, a Place can be a remembered entity, a virtual (real but not present) entity, or an imagined entity that we mentally place at some location – by pointing to it or by placing it at the location; the latter operation is also a common grammatical operation used in signed languages, as we will see in Section 4.2.

One unification suggested by this account is that the set of Places along the continuum in Figure 6 subsumes the traditional distinction made between deixis and anaphora. Talmy (2018, p. 1) writes that "Broadly, an anaphoric referent is an element of the current discourse, whereas a deictic referent is outside the discourse in the spatiotemporal surroundings. This is a distinction made between the lexical and the physical, one that has traditionally led to distinct theoretical treatments of the corresponding referents." Talmy proposes an alternative: "language engages the same cognitive system to single out a referent whether it is speech-internal or speech-external." Like Talmy, we suggest that these two domains of reference are manifestations of the same conceptual system. Further, because signed languages are expressed in space, and in a great many constructions both deictic referents and anaphoric referents are associated with locations in space, we find no need to impose a distinction between these types of locations. Conceptually and phonologically they are part of the same linguistic system and manifest as Place symbolic structures. We will take up this matter again in Section 7.

To summarize, Places are symbolic structures consisting of a schematic semantic pole (the most schematic meaning of Place is "thing") and a schematic phonological pole (a location in space). The baseline Place is a perceptible physical object. Through our experience with the world we construct networks of Places with varying degrees of semantic (what is the thing?) and phonological (where is it located?) schematicity/specificity. Cognitive abilities such as memory and imagination operate to yield elaborations of this baseline situation, with increased detachment from perception of the experiential world requiring increased conceptual resources. By using these general cognitive abilities and the linguistic resource of Places, signers are able to semantically instantiate and phonologically direct attention to an unlimited number of Places that refer to distinct discourse entities. Obviously, this analysis is valid for gesturers as well. This does not mean that signs are gestures, just as a dynamic systems model can account for both linguistic and nonlinguistic skilled movements (Hawkins 1992; Saltzman & Kelso 2009). We will discuss the issue of what counts as a sign and what counts as a gesture in Section 7.

Pointing Device

The other symbolic component of pointing constructions is the pointing device. In previous work we have characterized the schematic meaning of pointing devices as *directing attention* (Wilcox & Occhino, 2016). How is this accomplished? Conceptually, a pointing construction selects a particular referent from a pool of candidate entities in our mental universe. It does so by mentally pointing to the selected entity (the arrow in Figure 7), thereby profiling (bolded) it as the focus of attention and indicating its status relative to the ground (G). This candidate pool (large circle) and the potential referents (small circles) are elements of the semantic pole of the pointing device. Semantically, the pointing device does not make reference to a specific referent; rather, the selected referent is a schematic dependent structure internal to the pointing device's semantic pole (cross-hatching in Figure 7 indicates schematicity). This schematic structure must be elaborated, and this is the function of the semantic pole of a Place, depicted by the right portion of Figure 7.

The pointing device is a grounding element that indicates the epistemic status of the referent Place in relation to the ground. The grounding function of the pointing device is further elaborated in Figure 8. The ground (G) is offstage, although part of the conceptual maximal scope. The pointing device as grounding element directs attention to a schematic dependent semantic structure and puts it onstage as the focus of attention in the immediate scope. The Place component corresponds to (dotted line) and elaborates (arrow) the schematic focus of attention (schematicity here indicated by gray hashing). The composite level is shown at the top of Figure 8. The pointing device as grounding element directs attention to and profiles the specific referent instantiated by the Place.

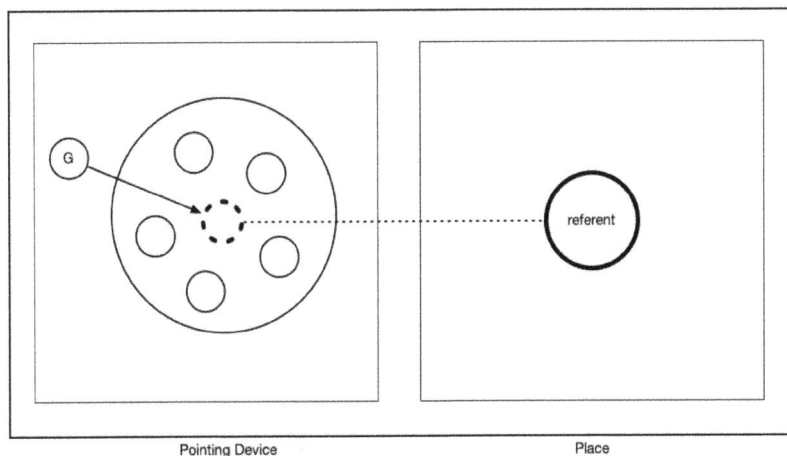

Pointing Device   Place

Figure 7 Pointing device semantic pole

Pointing Construction

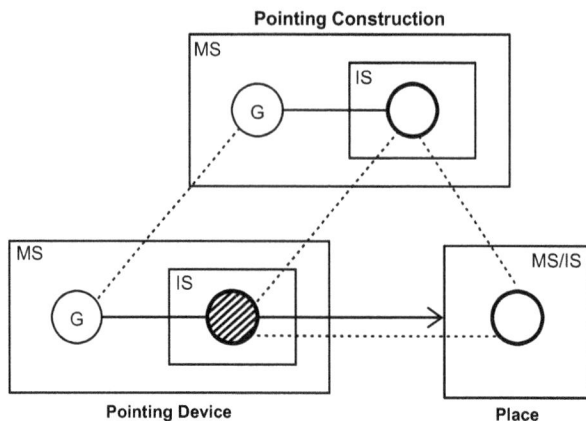

Figure 8 Pointing device as grounding element

We have simplified the description in a way that requires a more detailed explanation. When we say that the semantic pole of Place instantiates and elaborates the schematic element profiled in the semantic pole of the pointing device, the way this happens depends on the context of use. When we point to a physically present cappuccino cup, the semantic pole of Place is directly instantiated by the cup. In other uses, the semantic pole of Place is itself also schematic ("thing"), and has to be elaborated elsewhere in the discourse. Thus, the bottom portion of Figure 8 may extend to other expressions in the discourse, and the final specification of the referent will depend on a chain of correspondences. This is further exemplified by proxy-antecedent constructions (see Figure 11).

In summary, the semantic pole of the pointing device makes internal reference to a dependent element, mentally directing attention to it. This dependent element is elaborated by the semantic pole of a Place symbolic structure. The referent is either directly specified, or it is specified elsewhere in the discourse through a chain of correspondences. The pointing device is a grounding element, specifying the profiled referent schematically and putting it onstage as the profiled focus of attention. The referent, the semantic pole of the Place, is what the pointing device profiles in the composite pointing construction.

Pointing Constructions in Signed Languages

Pointing is a ubiquitous feature of the world's signed languages. Pointing signs function as "deictic and anaphoric pronouns, possessive and reflexive pronouns, demonstratives, locatives, determiners, body part labels, and verb agreement" (Meier & Lillo-Martin 2013, p. 151). Here we will examine anaphoric pronouns.

One aspect of grounding that pronouns must accomplish is locating the referent in relation to the ground. Another factor is singling out a unique referent. In the case of first- and second-person pronouns, both of these factors are intrinsic, since they single out referents inherent to the ground, the speaker/ signer and the addressee. A more difficult problem is raised by third-person pronouns. It is possible that many referents are available in the current discourse. To be used felicitously, a third-person anaphoric pronoun must uniquely identify an antecedent referent. For example, if someone says *My new Honda CR-V is a hybrid. It is the first hybrid I have ever owned*, the interlocutor must identify the full nominal in the prior discourse to which *it* refers.

The CG description of the semantics of pronominal anaphora relies on conceptual reference point relationships (Langacker, 1993; Langacker 2000; Van Hoek 1997). The reference point relationship is shown in Figure 9, in which C is the conceptualizer; R is the reference point, a salient entity in the current discourse space; T is the target structure to which R provides access; and D is the dominion, the set of potential targets. A spatial example of a reference point occurs when someone says, "The linguistics department is directly across from the library"; the reference point is the library and the target is the linguistics department. The dominion is all the possible targets that may be located relative to the reference point.

For anaphoric pronouns (Figure 10) the semantic pole of a pronoun profiles a schematic thing (indicated by ellipses in the target). It also incorporates the assumption that the speech act participants have mental access to the intended referent, the full nominal antecedent which serves as the pronoun's reference point. Mental access is provided by the reference point relationship (indicated by the dashed arrow): the pronoun target is in the dominion of the reference

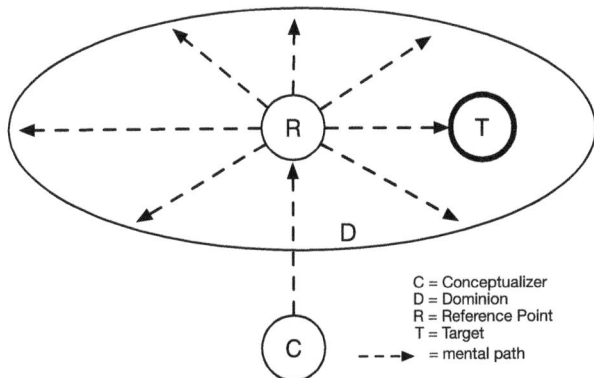

C = Conceptualizer
D = Dominion
R = Reference Point
T = Target
- - -▶ = mental path

Figure 9 Reference point
(Wilcox & Occhino, 2016)

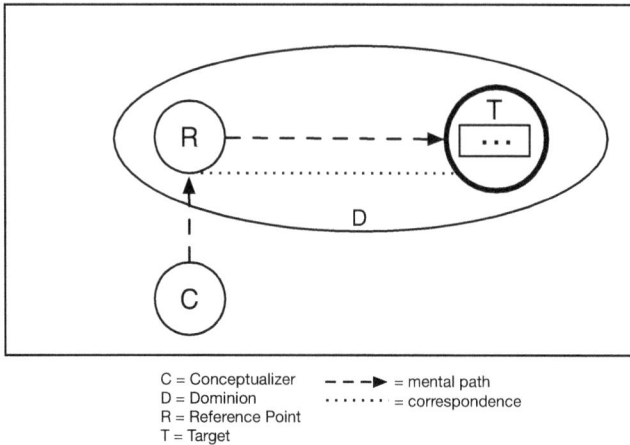

Figure 10 Antecedent-anaphor relation
(from Wilcox & Occhino, 2016)

point antecedent, which is presumed to be salient and accessible to the inter-locutors in the current discourse context. From the addressee's perspective, an anaphor gives instructions to seek a prominent entity which serves as the target's reference in the current discourse context.

The reference point analysis of the relationship between anaphoric pronouns and antecedents applies to signed languages as well, with one exception. In the Honda CR-V example, there are two elements: the antecedent (*my Honda CR-V*) and the anaphor (*it*). A similar antecedent-anaphor construction in a signed language often requires three elements: the antecedent, a proxy antecedent, and the anaphoric pronoun.

For example, in Australian Sign Language (Auslan), a narrator signs a noun, TEACHER, which is then followed by a pointing sign directed to a particular location on the right of the signer, establishing an association between the referent and the right side of the signing space. Later in the narrative, the signer again points to the location on the right to refer to the teacher. Expressions such as this are common in signed languages and indicate antecedent anaphor relations (Johnston & Schembri 2007, pp. 271–272).

In our CG analysis, a Place symbolic structure conventionally associates a referent with a phonological location in signing space. In the Auslan example, this is a location on the right side of the signer. The semantic pole of the Place symbolic structure profiles a schematic thing, which is associated with and elaborated by the semantic pole of the antecedent TEACHER. This Place thus serves as a proxy antecedent for TEACHER. In proxy-antecedent constructions the signer does not point directly to the lexical antecedent TEACHER, but to the phonological location of the proxy antecedent Place. In Figure 11, the semantic poles of the antecedent (TEACHER) and the proxy antecedent are connected by correspondence lines because the two are the same entity: the antecedent TEACHER instantiates the schematic semantic pole of the proxy antecedent Place. Later in the narrative, the signer again points to this proxy-antecedent Place; here the pointing construction designates a pronominal anaphor. The entity designated by the semantic pole of the Place component of this pointing construction, and the entity that semantically instantiated the Place component of the prior proxy antecedent – the lexical sign TEACHER – are conceptually mapped to the same entity as indicated by the correspondence lines. The anaphor, the proxy antecedent, and the antecedent (TEACHER) conceptually overlap: they are *co-referential*.

Proxy-antecedent constructions exhibit a unique feature only partially seen in spoken language antecedent-anaphor constructions. In most reference point constructions, the target is distinct from the reference point. In the previous example of the linguistics department and the library, the reference point (library) and target (linguistics department) are distinct entities. In anaphor-antecedent constructions, however, the reference point and the target are co-referential – *my Honda CR-V* and *it*, and TEACHER and the second pointing construction in Figure 11 are conceptually the same entity. Langacker (2000, p. 238) describes this as a *degenerate* reference point relationship: the reference point (antecedent) and the target (pronoun) collapse to a single entity in conceptual space (indicated by the correspondence line connecting the two in Figure 11). In signed languages, this conceptual degeneracy is expressed symbolically by *phonological* degeneracy: the phonological location of the proxy antecedent and the phonological location of anaphor – both of which are Place structures – coincide.

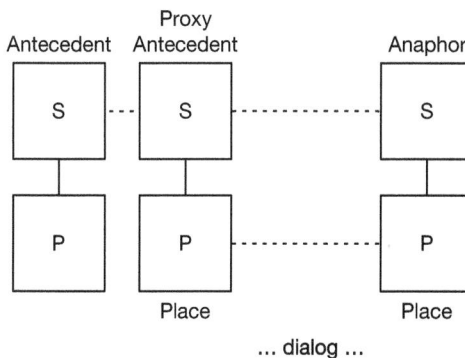

Figure 11 Proxy-antecedent anaphor construction
(Martínez & Wilcox, 2019)

The same phonological location across two or more symbolic structures is a common grammatical device used in many signed languages. This is a unique manifestation of Behaghel's law, the principle that elements that belong together semantically tend to be placed together syntactically. Langacker (1987) observes that the most straightforward kind of togetherness is linear juxtaposition, where one structure is placed immediately adjacent to another structure.[7] That is true for spoken languages, but for signed languages an even more straightforward kind of togetherness is possible: placement of the phonological poles of two structures at the same spatial location.

Placing

In addition to being components in pointing constructions, Places are also components in **placing** expressions. The term placing was introduced by Clark (2003, p. 185), who identified pointing and placing as two forms of gestural indicating, that is, of creating indexes for things. In pointing, speakers direct their addressee's attention to the object they are indicating. In placing, "speakers try to place the object they are indicating so that it falls within the addressees' focus of attention" (2003, p. 187). Clark offered the example of purchasing items in a drugstore: a customer identifies the items to be purchased by placing them on the counter, and then identifies the payment by placing cash on the counter.

Martínez and Wilcox (2019) extended the concept of placing in the context of signed languages. First, they observed that in signed language constructions, signs are communicative objects that can be placed in spatial locations. Second, they identified two types of placing: **create-placing**, in which a new Place is created, and **recruit-placing**, in which the signer recruits an existing Place. Figure 12 depicts a generic placing construction. S is the signer, I is the interlocutor, and G is the ground. The bold line with ball end indicates the act of placing. The dashed line with a magnet end indicates the subtle distinction between pointing and create-placing: rather than directing attention, create-placing locates an entity so that it falls within the addressee's focus of attention, and thus *attracts the attention* of the interlocutor to the Place.

An example of placing in Argentine Sign Language (LSA) is given in Martínez and Wilcox (2019). The signer introduces the biography of José de San Martín, a hero of the independence of Argentina, Chile, and Peru. At the beginning of the discourse a noun, PERSON, is create-placed at the right side of the signer, creating a new Place (Figure 13). The schematic semantic pole of the Place is elaborated by the semantic pole of PERSON, and the schematic phonological pole of the Place is elaborated by the location on the right of the

---

[7] In CG, temporal ordering is a dimension of phonological structure (Langacker 1987).

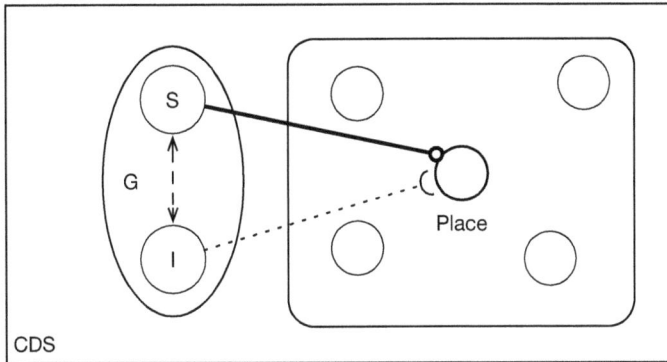

Figure 12 Placing
(Martínez & Wilcox, 2019)

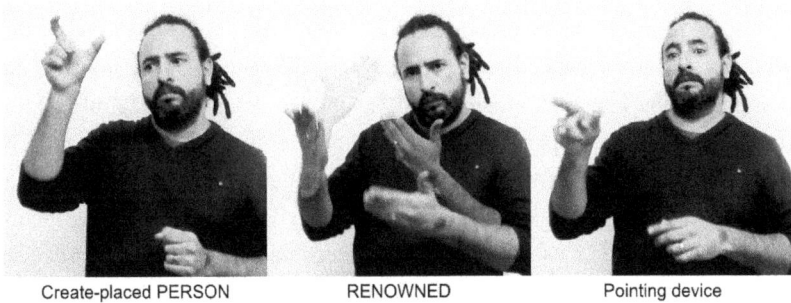

Create-placed PERSON   RENOWNED   Pointing device

Figure 13 Create-placed PERSON and Point
(Martínez & Wilcox, 2019)

signer. Constructions specific to a signed language often specify phonological locations for new Places, for example, perhaps specifying that new discourse entities are introduced on the signer's dominant side as we see here. The placing construction locates PERSON as a newly introduced referent intersubjectively identified and accessible to the interlocutors, and thus a grounded (but still indefinite) nominal.

Once the referent Place is created, the signer is able to refer to it in subsequent discourse. For instance, the sign RENOWNED (Figure 13) incorporates the nominal referent "person" as a participant of the adjectival relation by directing the sign toward the "person" Place. RENOWNED profiles one focal participant and associates the property of being famous with San Martín. Later in the discourse, the signer refers anaphorically to the same referent with pointing constructions (glossed as POINT(location)) directed to the Place instantiated by San Martín.

Pointing and placing are used to ground and track nominals at multiple levels of structure, from clauses to larger constructions. An example of more complex use of pointing comes from a video in LSA of the official account of the Argentine Deaf Movement or, in Spanish, Movimiento Argentino de Sordos (MAS) in support of a bill recognizing Argentine Sign Language. Among other political actions, the National Association of the Deaf in Argentina (CAS, Confederación Argentina de Sordos) organized an event at the National Congress building that gathered together more than 5,000 people. In the video, released two days before the event, two deaf leaders of the Movement, Alejandro Makotrinsky and Pablo Lemmo, make the point that the MAS movement should not attempt to label or classify hearing people as inherently wrong or bad.

Pablo then introduces what will become the overall topic: widespread ideology leads hearing people to believe that deaf people are mentally challenged, not equal, or are deaf-mute. He does this by first signing IDEOLOGY, a two-handed sign with a location at the head (Figure 14). Then, while his nondominant hand is still in the head location for IDEOLOGY, he begins to point to it with his dominant hand. More precisely, by the time Pablo completes the pointing action his nondominant hand has moved down to a neutral position (as seen in the second panel of Figure 14), and so the sign IDEOLOGY is no longer present (like the missing cappuccino cup), and so he is pointing to the spatial location formerly occupied by IDEOLOGY. This pointing construction grounds IDEOLOGY as a nominal and creates an ideology-Place. However, rather than simply pointing up to the sign (since its location is high in signing space), Pablo reaches his pointing arm up above the sign and points down at it. Downward pointing in LSA, and possibly in other signed languages, has been shown to express proximal meaning (Martínez & Wilcox, 2019). Here, Pablo wants to create a sense of conceptual closeness with the concept of ideology,

IDEOLOGY   Pointing Device   CHANGE

Figure 14 IDEOLOGY pointing and recruit-placing
(Martínez & Wilcox, 2019)

emphasizing that "**this** thing we call ideology, **this** is what we have to attend to and focus on." Pablo articulates the pointing device with several forceful reduplicated movements. It has also been shown that increased directive force can be expressed in various ways in LSA (Martínez & Wilcox, 2019), including reduplicated movements of the pointing device directed at the referent Place. Pablo then continues.

To express the idea that the goal is to change society's ideology pertaining to deaf people, Pablo recruit-places the sign CHANGE in the newly created ideology-Place (Figure 14). In this construction, CHANGE is unspecified for phonological location; the schematic location of CHANGE is elaborated by the location of the ideology-Place, which has been previously elaborated by the phonological location of IDEOLOGY. CHANGE profiles an action chain, which includes an unexpressed agent and a theme, the changed entity. In this construction, the theme is elaborated by the ideology-Place, which in turn conceptually maps to IDEOLOGY.

Figure 15 shows IDEOLOGY (a) and the ideology-Place (b) created by the pointing construction. IDEOLOGY is a lexical noun with full phonological specification (HC is hand configuration, MOV is movement), including the head location. IDEOLOGY is grounded as a full nominal by the proximal (downward directed) pointing device, which also creates an ideology-Place. IDEOLOGY thus corresponds to and elaborates the schematic Place. CHANGE is then recruit-placed at the location of the ideology-Place, indicating that "ideology" is the theme (TH), the changed entity. CHANGE is shown as a construction consisting of two symbolic structures: the action chain process "change" (double arrow) and the theme "ideology." CHANGE incorporates a schematic symbolic substructure (indicated by the rectangle enclosing the theme (TH) and

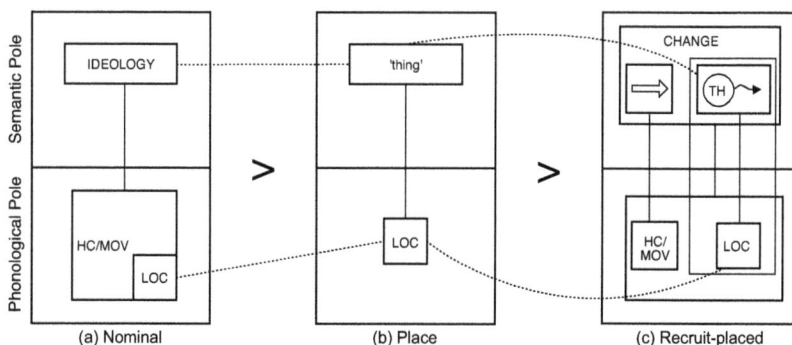

Figure 15 CHANGE recruit-placed
(Martínez & Wilcox, 2019)

the location (LOC). The semantic pole of this symbolic substructure specifies the theme. The schematic phonological pole is elaborated by the placing construction. Once again, we see double overlap of conceptual mapping and phonological mapping of Place symbolic structures.

4.2 Place and Placing in Agreement Constructions

Kibrik (2019, p. 76) has observed that "In modern linguistics, 'agreement' has developed into an entangled and incoherent notion." The entanglement and incoherence extends to and is amplified in discussions of agreement in signed languages (Cysouw 2011; Fischer & Gough, 1978; Liddell 2000b; Lillo-Martin & Meier 2011; Quer 2011; Schembri et al. 2018). Kibrik categorizes approaches to agreement in spoken languages into two types: a form-to-form approach, and a cognition-to-form-mapping approach. The traditional form-to-form approach claims that an agreement feature originates in one linguistic element, the controller, and is copied onto another one, the target. As Kibrik points out, the form-to-form approach presents several difficulties. For example, sometimes the agreement marker has nothing to agree with, or expresses entirely different information (Barlow 1999; Croft 2013; Langacker 2008).

In the cognition-to-form-mapping approach, agreement features are associated with referents in the cognitive representation. They serve to specify referents and are thus referential features which are mapped onto various sites in linguistic structure. The roots of agreement, according to Kibrik (2019, p. 37), "lie in cognitively motivated discourse processes associated with reference." Such an approach is also offered by Croft, who suggests it is possible to treat agreement affixes as expressing a symbolic relation (rather than a syntactic relation) indexing the referent, and thus to treat agreement as "double indexation" (Croft 2001, p. 229).

Agreement in CG is analyzed as **multiple symbolization**: "That is, information about some entity is symbolized by more than one component structure within the same symbolic assembly and thus has multiple manifestations in a single complex expression" (Langacker 2008, p. 188). Agreement in this view is "simply a matter of the same information being symbolized in multiple places. As such, it is just a special case of conceptual overlap, which is characteristic of all grammatical constructions" (Langacker 2008, p. 347). We rely on the CG account and analyze agreement as a special type of **conceptual overlap**: the same information is symbolized in multiple manifestations of symbolic structures that map to the same cognitive referent. The predominant way conceptual overlap is symbolized in these constructions is with phonological overlap: the double overlap we have already described.

We have already seen examples of multiple symbolization in the use of Place. In Figure 13, the sign RENOWNED incorporates the referent "person" as a participant of the adjectival relation by directing the sign toward the "person" Place, profiling the focal participant, San Martín, who had been associated with that Place in a previous discourse frame. The sign RENOWNED, in our analysis, contains a schematic symbolic substructure. Semantically, the substructure is specified as the antecedent of "renowned." The phonological pole of the substructure is specified as the end location of the movement path. In the example, this schematic substructure is phonologically elaborated by being placed at the location of the San Martín-Place. "Agreement" is thus manifest as two symbolic structures, or multiple symbolization: the schematic symbolic structure internal to RENOWN maps to the San Martín-Place symbolic structure, which elaborates its semantic and phonological poles.

A verbal example appears in Figure 14. Pablo has created an ideology-Place with a pointing construction. He then placed the sign CHANGE at the ideology-Place. In this construction, the semantic pole of CHANGE contains a schematic substructure specifying the theme of the verb "change" and a schematic phonological pole, both of which must be instantiated. In the placing construction, the schematic semantic substructure is instantiated by the semantic pole of the ideology-Place, which in turn corresponds to "ideology." The schematic phonological location is instantiated by the phonological location of the ideology-Place, which corresponds to the phonological location of "ideology." Again, we find that multiple symbolic Place structures map to the same conceptual entity, "ideology."

In the same Movimiento Argentino de Sordos video, Pablo produces another agreement form. Continuing his narrative, Pablo explains that because of their ideology, hearing people regard deaf people as mentally challenged, not equal to hearing people, mute, and incapable. Prior to this segment, Pablo had placed the sign CHANGE directed toward himself, recruiting his body as a Place symbolic structure to represent people in general; in this context, it is clear that he refers to hearing people who have negative attitudes toward deaf people. Even though he is actually deaf, Pablo uses this argumentative strategy because he wants to convince hearing people to change their negative view of deaf people without directly confronting them.

Pablo again produces the sign PERSON with his nondominant hand, placing the sign at the spatial location occupied by Alejandro – in other words, at the Alejandro-Place. This placing construction is a component in a larger, simultaneous construction (Figure 16). While Pablo continues to hold the placed sign PERSON, he signs DEAF TO-SEE DEAF with his dominant hand. The verb TO-SEE is produced with a path movement from Pablo toward Alejandro.

Simultaneous construction PERSON TO-SEE

Figure 16 Simultaneous placing construction

Pablo then lists the negative characteristics that hearing people perceive deaf people as having. TO-SEE in the sense used here is not a perceptual verb; rather, it is a verb of cognitive activity. TO-SEE means "to regard as" or "to think of," and in this use it expresses the cognitive activity of hearing people categorizing deaf people.

The lexical sign PERSON is a type specification. When placed, it integrates the "person" type with the semantic pole of the Alejandro-Place. However, the semantic pole of this Place is not Alejandro. Rather, Alejandro's Place serves as a reference point, affording mental access to a dominion of targets. We have previously shown that reference point constructions in signed languages are used to associate characteristics or properties as reference point targets with referents (Martínez & Wilcox 2019), in this case, characteristics associated with Alejandro. The targets could be Alejandro's gender, his hair color, his clothing, or any number of other characteristics. In this situation, the most salient target is Alejandro's deafness. This characteristic is explicitly mentioned when Pablo signs DEAF TO-SEE DEAF. As shown in the lower portion in Figure 17, the PERSON component integrates with the Alejandro-Place component, specifically the target "deaf" of the reference point, to create the composite construction "deaf people."

This composite construction is then a component in a higher-level construction that integrates "deaf people" with TO-SEE. TO-SEE has two schematic symbolic substructures: the categorizer and the object of categorization. These two substructures are elaborated by Place structures. The semantic element of the categorizer substructure is elaborated in the prior discourse frame when Pablo uses the placing construction to present himself as a hearing person. Pablo is making the point that hearing people are doing the categorization. The semantic element of the second substructure, the object of categorization, is elaborated by the composite construction "deaf people," producing the complex construction "hearing people see deaf people" as incapable, and so on. The middle portion of Figure 17 shows that the component "deaf people" conceptually elaborates and

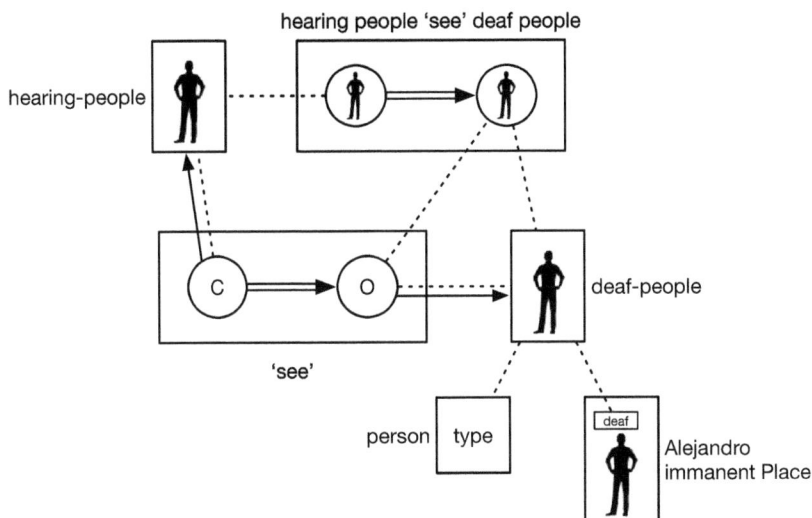

Figure 17 Simultaneous placing construction

corresponds to the schematic object of conceptualization element (O) of TO-SEE. The component "hearing people" conceptually corresponds to and elaborates the schematic conceptualizer (C), and integrates with the component "deaf people" to yield the final composite construction "hearing people 'see' deaf people."

The phonological side of these constructions shows comparable complexity. The relevant issue is the location of the Place structures. The phonological location of PERSON is schematic, allowing it to be placed. When PERSON is placed in this context, the phonological location of the Alejandro-Place elaborates the schematic phonological location of PERSON. The phonological poles of the two schematic substructures of TO-SEE are also elaborated by Places. The Pablo-Place (representing hearing people) elaborates the phonological location of the first schematic substructure, the categorizer. The schematic phonological location of the second substructure, the object of categorization, is elaborated by the phonological location of the Alejandro-Place (representing deaf people).

Observe that both groups are virtual: no actual hearing or deaf people are involved, although both are expressed by Places occupied by real people in the spatial environment. The virtual deaf people are evoked by Alejandro's Place when integrated with the type specification PERSON. The conceptualizer of TO-SEE is also a Place (Pablo's) created by the placing construction in the previous discourse frame to create virtual hearing people. Thus, Places associated with physical entities – Pablo and Alejandro and their spatial locations in the ground – play essential roles in the component structures that form this complex grammatical construction referring to virtual groups of people. This use of Places that correspond to physical entities in the spatial environment has been described for other grammatical expressions in LSA (Martínez & Wilcox 2019; Wilcox & Martínez 2020) and appears to be common to other signed languages as well. That signers can use Places associated with physical entities in the spatial environment is a manifestation of the Place continuum. It is not, however, generally accepted that the grammars of signed languages are capable of incorporating real-world locations in the discourse ground in this way. We will discuss this issue more in Section 7.

A final example of multiple symbolization and conceptual overlap in LSA occurs in a narrative about a famous event in Argentina. The signer says, "This man, Lagomarsino, the one who gave the gun to Nisman … " The signer first points to a location in front and slightly to her right, creating a Place, which for the moment remains schematic: we don't know what or who this Place refers to. She then signs MAN, a body-anchored sign produced at the mouth. Next, she places the sign PERSON at the newly created Place. She then fingerspells the name Lagomarsino followed by a relative marker meaning "the one who" directed at the Place. Finally, she signs an agreement verb GIVE, moving from the Place to a location on her left.

Figure 18 diagrams this excerpt. The solid line (a) is the first pointing construction which creates a Place (b). Line (c) represents the placing of PERSON. Line (d) depicts the relative marker directed at the Place. Finally, circle (e) shows the initial location of the verb GIVE (indicated by an arrow), and (f) shows the final location.

Figure 19 depicts the semantic pole of the structures in this discourse segment. The arrows indicate the appearance of Place structures across the segment. A semantically schematic Place is created by pointing. Body-anchored MAN elaborates the entity type; we now know that the Place refers to a man.

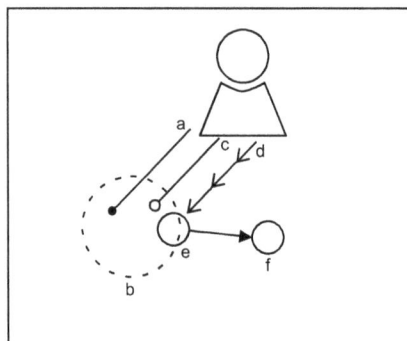

Figure 18 Lagomarsino discourse segment

Place	Man	PERSON	"Lagomarsino"	Relative marker	GIVE
Semantically schematic (created by pointing)	Type elaboration of Place	Placed	Fingerspelled name fully elaborates semantic pole	Recruit-placed Identifies antecedent of relative clause "the one who…"	Recruit-placed initial location (agent)

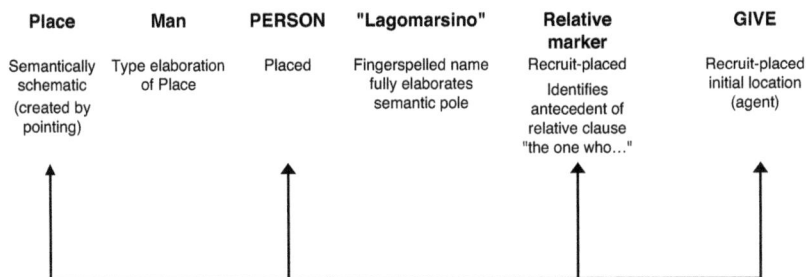

Figure 19 Lagomarsino semantic pole

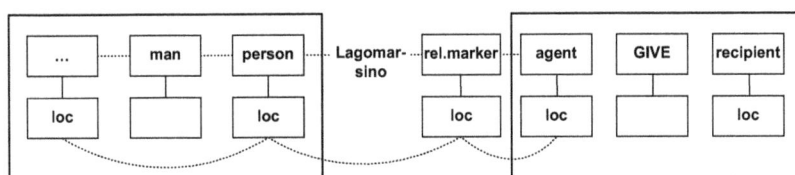

Figure 20 Lagomarsino semantic and phonological poles

PERSON, placed at the man-Place, provides phonological substance to the location of the Place. Fingerspelled "Lagomarsino" fully elaborates the Place: we now know the referent of the Place. The relative marker, recruit-placed at the Lagomarsino-Place, tells us that the referent at this Place is the one who will be doing something. Finally, we learn that Lagomarsino gave a gun (to the person who will be described in the subsequent discourse frame). The initial phonological location of GIVE is placed at the Lagomarsino-Place.

Figure 20 depicts the semantic and phonological correspondences. The semantic poles of the initial Place, MAN, PERSON, Lagomarsino, the head of the relative markers, and the agent of GIVE correspond – they map to the same conceptual entity. At the bottom of the diagram, the phonological pole correspondences are shown: the initial Place, PERSON, the head of the relative marker, and the agent of GIVE all are produced in the same spatial location. MAN is body-anchored and thus has a different phonological location (near the mouth), and Lagomarsino is fingerspelled at a location in neutral signing space.[8]

In summary, these examples demonstrate grammatical constructions characterized by multiple symbolization and conceptual overlap. We also see that in these constructions, conceptual overlap is achieved by **phonological overlap**: the phonological poles across multiple symbolic structures are articulated at the same location in space, the phonological location of a corresponding Place structure.

---

[8] Fingerspelling can, in fact, be placed, but it is not in this example.

Conceptual Space

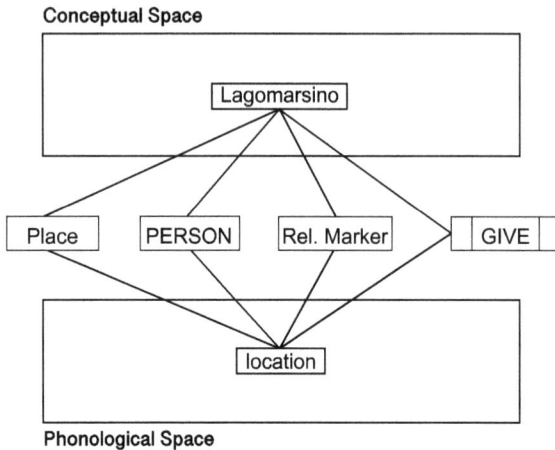

Phonological Space

Figure 21 Double overlap in multiple symbolization

This double overlap for the Lagomarsino example is shown in Figure 21. The initial Place structure (created by a pointing construction), placed PERSON, the relative marker, and the initial symbolic substructure (agent) of GIVE all map to the same entity in conceptual space – Lagomarsino. They also map to the same location in phonological space.

Not all uses of GIVE and similar verbs require full elaboration of each schematic substructure. GIVE may appear in constructions where the agent substructure is left unspecified. For example, if a signer reports that he took his car to a shop and received a bill for the repairs, he might sign GIVE so that the initial location is distal from the signer, moving toward and ending at the signer. This would express a passive meaning, "a bill was given to me," where the agent of "give" is left unspecified and nondeployable in subsequent discourse (Janzen et al. 2001). The initial location is phonologically elaborated by a conventional Place in the grammar of ASL, the distal location. The semantic pole of this distal Place is a schematic "thing" with no further elaboration; when it integrates with the initial substructure of GIVE, which has only semantic specification of agent, the composite symbolic assembly leaves the agent unspecified and defocused – characteristics of passive constructions. The ending substructure is semantically and phonologically elaborated by the signer Place: the signer is the recipient of the bill. This is also an example of multiple symbolization and conceptual overlap. The essential difference between this use and the Lagomarsino use is that in this construction, the initial substructure of GIVE remains semantically unspecified except for its status as agent.

In the next section we show that signs are not the only communicative objects that can be placed. The signer is also a symbolic structure that can be placed, again resulting in conceptual and phonological overlap.

4.3 Placing the Signer in Reported Dialogue

Dialogue in narrative can be presented either as a third-person report (indirect quotation) or as first-person ("direct quotation") (Chafe 1982). Tannen (1986) points out that what is referred to as reported speech or direct quotation is actually constructed dialogue. Speakers mark these constructed dialogues with certain conventional grammatical constructions, or by taking on the voices of characters by changes in pitch, voice quality, and prosody (Schiffrin 1981; Tannen 1986). In doing so, the speaker takes the point of view of a character in the narrative.

Just as speakers have ways of presenting a point of view by taking on the vocal and behavioral qualities of characters, signers use their whole bodies and the space surrounding them to convey viewpoint in reported dialogue. Padden (1986) offers an example, depicted in Figure 22. The signer says, "The husband goes, 'Really, I didn't mean it'." In the first frame the signer faces her actual interlocutor and signs HUSBAND, identifying who will be speaking in the next sequence. The next four frames present the constructed dialogue REALLY ME NOT MEAN "Really, I didn't mean it" as signed by the husband. To mark the constructed dialogue, the signer shifts her body to the right and directs her eye gaze at the husband's virtual addressee.

Constructions such as this that are used for expressing quotations from a character viewpoint have received different names in the sign linguistic literature, such as role shift (Padden 1986; Quer 2016), shifted reference (Engberg-Pedersen 1993), and constructed action (Cormier et al. 2013; Ferrara & Johnston 2014; Metzger 1995). Descriptions of these constructions in signed languages tend to include one or more of these phonological features: (i) a change in body orientation (the signer changes orientation, for instance, from front position to a sideways position); (ii) a change in eye gaze direction (the signer tends to break eye contact from the actual addressee to look in another direction, such as the

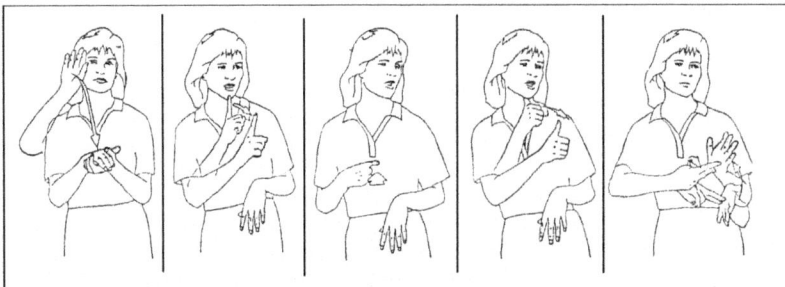

Figure 22 Role shift
(Padden 1986)

location of virtual character or referent within discourse); (iii) and a change in deixis (the deictic center, the body of the signer, is rearranged to take somebody else's point of view). As Engberg-Pedersen (1993) has observed, these constructions also co-occur with some or all of the following semantic features: (i) shifted reference: the use of pronouns to refer to somebody other than the sender/narrator; (ii) shifted attribution of expressive elements: the use of the signer's face and/or body posture to express emotions or attitudes of somebody other than the sender/narrator in the context of utterance; and (iii) shifted locus: the use of the sender/narrator locus for somebody other than the sender/narrator.

In Section 3 we introduced the stage model. One aspect of the stage model is **viewing arrangement**, defined as the overall relationship between the "viewers" and the situation "viewed" (Langacker 2008). Within CG, the term "viewers" refers to conceptualizers who apprehend the meanings of linguistic expressions; they are the signer/speaker and the addressee. In a communicative event, the viewers are the speaker/signer and interlocutor. In the default viewing arrangement (Figure 23), the viewer is offstage while the object of perception (P) is onstage (OS) within the overall field of perception. The default viewing arrangement also reflects the asymmetry between what is viewed, the *object of conceptualization*, and the viewer, the *subject of conceptualization* (Langacker 1991a). When this asymmetry is fully polarized, as in the default viewing arrangement, the subject of conception is construed with maximal subjectivity, as the viewer fully attending to the object of perception in the objective scene; the viewer is not a part of that scene and has no awareness of self as viewer. In an alternative construal, the viewer moves onstage and may even become the focused object of conceptualization. Expressions which explicitly reference the ground, such as the signer/speaker

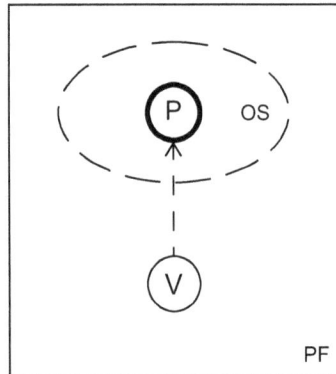

Figure 23 Default viewing arrangement
(Langacker 1991a)

or the interlocutor, such as *I*, *me*, and *you*, manifest this viewing arrangement. Other aspects of the ground which are normally off-stage can be moved onstage with words such as *now* or *here*.

It is important to note that while viewing arrangement is experientially grounded in the embodied link between *perception* and *conception*, the stage model and viewing arrangement pertain to conceptualizations: they characterize the meaning of linguistic expressions, the semantic pole of symbolic structures. For both spoken and signed languages, these cognitive models pertain to semantic structure.

In signed language discourse the stage model and viewing arrangement retain their physical, experiential, and perceptual grounding. This is seen when signers present narrative, either in person or more and more frequently on social media: a signer as narrator literally occupies a location on a stage that is visually perceived by the interlocutor as audience. In the default narrative arrangement, the signer and any interactional partners virtually represented through reported speech are on-stage participants, while the audience remains off-stage as viewer. In presenting narratives, the signer as narrator occupies a location; the narrator then assumes character roles in the narrative, interacting with other (virtual) participants. Thus, for signed languages, the stage model and viewing arrangement are aspects of both meaning and form. The signer, the signer's location "on stage," and the relation of the signer to the viewers have phonological significance.

We have shown that the signer may function as a symbolic structure. When Pablo places the sign PERSON directed at Alejandro, he recruits Alejandro as a symbolic structure, a Place, integrating certain aspects of the Alejandro-Place with the person type to form the composite expression "deaf people." In this construction, both the sign PERSON and a person in the discourse context, Alejandro, are symbolic components that integrate to form a composite structure. The signer can also move about, occupying different meaningful locations. In these cases the signer is a symbolic structure which can be placed, either to create a Place or to recruit an existing Place. We call constructions of this type **placing the signer**. We analyze the formal changes the signer makes in narrative reporting of dialogue and events – that is, changes in body orientation, eye gaze, and deixis – to be instances of placing the signer.

As always, the visual nature of signed languages influences both form and meaning. Signed languages are, quite literally, face-to-face visual languages. In signed language interaction, the canonical communication configuration is for one signer to face another signer at some culturally determined distance. Between the two is a line of sight. We call this the **canonical interactional configuration** (CIC). The well-known Gricean cooperative principle and maxims of conversation describe how people achieve effective conversational communication (Grice 1989). Gricean maxims are focused on the content of the communicators' contributions to conversational interaction. For signed communication among deaf language users, two maxims for the production of effective visual communication also come into play: (1) reduce excessive moving around from the point of view of the interlocutor, and (2) make your signs as visible as possible.

When narrating a story, canonical conversational configuration and communicative maxims constrain the signer. The signer is not free to occupy any location whatsoever, and the signs must remain visible. Thus, in Figure 22, the signer does not move into the location of the virtual interlocutor who says, "Really, I didn't mean it." This would result in excessive movement, especially if the narrative were to continue with a dialogue between the narrator and the virtual interlocutor: the signer would have to constantly move back and forth between these locations. It also would result in the interlocutor facing the signer, making the signs nearly impossible to be seen by the audience. Instead, what we see are attenuated changes in body orientation and eye gaze. Together, these signal that the signer occupies a new location – in our analysis, the signer has been placed.

Figure 22 was an example of reported dialogue in conversational interaction. The same placing construction is used in narrative. Figure 24 is taken from a video documenting the Argentine folk story "The Golden Hand" about three sisters who face several challenges posed by a dangerous man whose hand has been cut off and replaced with a golden hand. Prior dialogue has established

Figure 24 Golden Hand Place
(Wilcox, Martínez & Morales 2022)

a second sister Place on her right, and the Golden Hand man is on her left. The signer as narrator begins by explaining that the Golden Hand man and one of the sisters are riding together in a horse-drawn carriage. The signer's body is in the conventional narrator Place in the center; her eye gaze and signing are oriented toward the viewing audience. In Figure 24, the narrator has been placed in the Golden Hand man Place. With his left hand the Golden Hand man keeps holding the reins of his horse; he signs with the right hand. The Golden Hand man asks: "Do you remember me? Some time ago I went to your place. There was a storm. Something happened and I lost my hand." The narrator's body moves to occupy a spatial position slightly on the left; eye gaze and signing are oriented toward the interlocutor, the sister Place, thus maintaining the canonical interactional configuration.

In Figure 25, the narrator has been placed to occupy a spatial location on the right, the sister Place; eye gaze and signing are oriented toward the Golden Hand man Place on the right. The sister then replies: "Hmm, you? Oh, yes, I remember you came here when there was a storm. Yes, I remember your face. You cut off your hand?"

It may not seem obvious at first why we analyze this strategy for expressing reported dialogue as placing the signer: how has the signer been spatially "placed" in the same way as PERSON was placed in Figure 13 or CHANGE in Figure 14? An instructional video designed to teach students of Brazilian Sign Language (Libras) how a single signer reports interactional dialogue, such as the Golden Hand narrative, illustrates how placing the signer works.

Figure 25 Sister Place
(Wilcox, Martínez & Morales 2022)

In this video the instructor, Eduardo, and his colleague, Leonardo, first demonstrate a signed dialogue as it would actually take place between two interlocutors, maintaining the face-to-face canonical interactional configuration (Figure 26).

Eduardo then shows how the same interaction would be presented by a single narrator with reported dialogue (Figure 27). The simplest and most realistic way for a narrator to present a two-person reported dialogue to an audience would be to "act out" the interaction by taking both roles on the phonological stage – that is, by simply recreating Figure 26, moving between the spatial locations of the two participants. This would, however, violate the visual communication maxims. Instead, Eduardo as the narrator remains essentially in one location, and by changing the orientation of his body, the narrator alternately assumes the role of Eduardo or Leonardo.

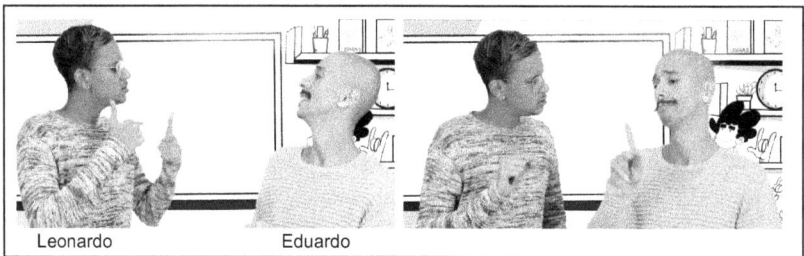

Figure 26 Demonstration of two person interaction
(Wilcox, Martínez & Morales 2022)

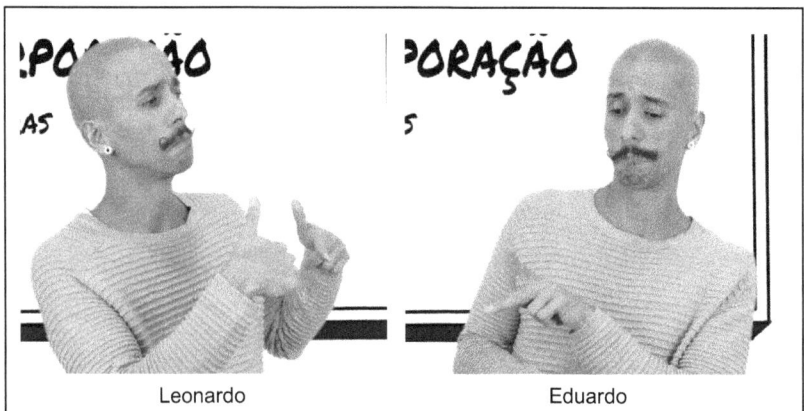

Figure 27 Narrated interaction
(Wilcox, Martínez & Morales 2022)

A diagrammatic representation of the real two-person interaction and the strategy in which the signer is placed is depicted in Figure 28. The top portion (A) shows the original interaction with Eduardo (E) on the right and Leonardo (L) on the left. The construction in which the signer is placed to express the reported interaction is depicted in the lower portion (B). When Eduardo as narrator (N) presents Eduardo's utterances in interaction with Leonardo, he rotates his orientation slightly to his right, indicating that he has assumed Eduardo's Place. Virtually present Leonardo assumes a position directly in front of Eduardo to maintain the canonical interactional configuration. When presenting Leonardo's utterances directed to Eduardo, Eduardo as narrator changes orientation in the opposite direction, thus indicating that the narrator has occupied the Leonardo Place; in doing so, he takes the role of Leonardo. Eduardo, as a virtual addressee, now assumes a position in front of Leonardo to maintain the canonical interactional configuration (CIC). Thus, the overall scene is presented with Eduardo "playing" himself and Leonardo, who are both alternatively presented as virtual versions of themselves (represented by the dashed circles).

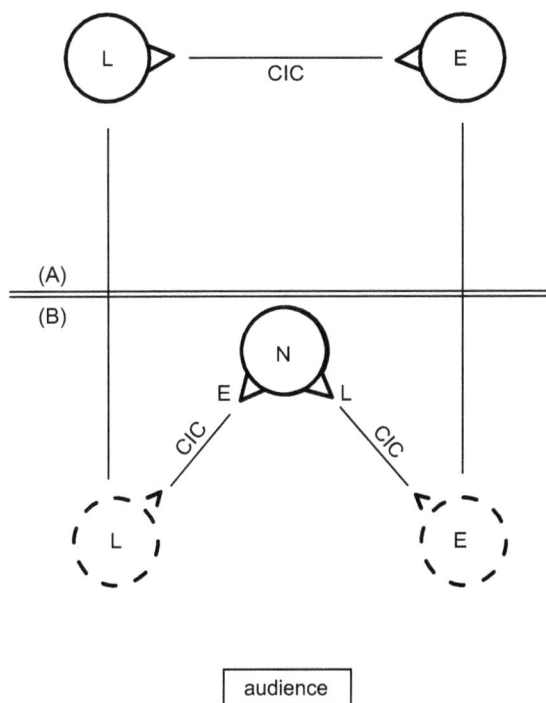

Figure 28 Placing the signer in reported dialog
(Wilcox, Martínez & Morales 2022)

In this instructional video we see the relation between a real two-person interaction and how a single narrator reports the interaction, maintaining the canonical interactional configuration while also abiding by the visual communication maxims. As it appears in the Golden Hand narrative, the placing construction closely aligns the phonological pole – the location – of the narrator with the phonological pole of the Golden Hand man. This conceptually maps the semantic pole of the narrator onto the semantic pole of the Golden Hand man. In nontechnical terms, we would say that the narrator "has become the Golden Hand" or "Eduardo has become Leonardo."

Constructions in which the signer is placed are used in narratives to indicate changes in character perspective. By placing the signer in the Place conventionally associated with the narrator, for example, the signer is conceptually mapped to the narrator. The same process occurs for mapping the narrator to character roles, as with the Golden Hand and Libras tutorial examples. Placing the signer appears in several other grammatical constructions across different signed languages, including fictive discourse and fictive interaction (Jarque & Pascual 2016); passive constructions in ASL (Janzen et al. 2001); and evidentiality (Jarque & Pascual 2015; Shaffer 2012; Wilcox & Shaffer 2017).

There is a great deal more semantic and phonological complexity in constructions of this type than we have described here. It is obvious from the figures in this section that the phonological expression of placing differs. When presenting reported or constructed dialogue in conversation as in Figure 22, we see very little change in spatial location; the markers of placing are primarily the change in body orientation and in gaze direction. In the tutorial shown in Figure 27, Eduardo demonstrates how to express reported dialog by change in body orientation and eye gaze, and also with more pronounced change in upper body positioning or leaning – thus the upper body changes location somewhat more than in conversational reporting. The Golden Hand folk story narrative is presented in a more dramatic style, and so spatial placing of the narrator is more pronounced. Other factors also come into play in various types of placing the signer constructions. One complicating factor is body partitioning (Dudis 2004). In body partitioning, different portions of the signer's body – hands, arms, head, mouth, eyes – may be used independently to represent different semantic content. Thus, it is possible for the signer's body and hands to occupy a Place phonologically associated with one particular conception, while the signer's head, eyes, and mouth occupy a different Place – looking in a different location than the one in which the body is oriented, for example – associated with a different conception. A body-partitioned double placing construction such as this might be used to simultaneously express a statement (body and hands) and the reaction to that statement by an unspecified or fictive other person (head, eyes, and mouth). It could also be used to express a statement by the signer and the signer's stance toward that statement. For example, the signer might state that deaf people find it difficult to be accepted into medical school in some countries; while signing this, the signer turns her head and looks to her right to express a fictive interaction in which her face displays her disdain for such a situation. Here, then, the signer has used body partitioning to place her body and hands in one Place that is conceptually mapped to the signer as reporter of the factual situation, and, by shifting her head orientation and eye gaze, she creates a new Place that represents a different conceptualization – her stance in regard to the situation.

Across these examples, we see that placing constructions express conceptual mapping. Placing brings into congruence the phonological pole of a symbolic structure, whether it is a sign or the signer, with the phonological pole of another symbolic structure, thereby putting the semantic poles of these structures in some type of correspondence. In reported dialog, the correspondence is that of referential identity: by placing the signer in the phonological location of the interlocutor in a reported dialog, the signer is conceptually mapped to the interlocutor. Placing is a manifestation in actual space of the conceptual metaphors SIMILARITY IS PROXIMITY and RELATEDNESS IS PROXIMITY, which we suggest is the conceptual basis of Behaghel's law discussed in Section 4.1. The spatial environment in which signed discourse is expressed is, in a real sense, a phonological stage on which placing constructions play out. While conceptual proximity certainly pertains to signed languages, proximity of spatial locations is an aspect of the phonology of signed languages.

5 Modality

Grammatical modality pertains to the semantic domain of necessity and possibility (Auwera & Plungian 1998; Nuyts & van der Auwera 2016). Modality is widely studied for spoken languages from a variety of linguistic theoretical approaches. Studies of signed language modality are less common and again adopt formalist, functional, and cognitive perspectives. Some of the signed languages on which research of modality has been reported include American Sign Language (Janzen & Shaffer 2002; Shaffer 2002; Shaffer, 2004; Wilcox 1996; Wilcox & Shaffer 2006; Wilcox & Wilcox 1995); Brazilian Sign Language (Brito 1990; Xavier & Wilcox 2014); Spanish Sign Language (Cabeza-Pereiro 2013; Herrero-Blanco & Salazar-García 2010; Iglesias-Lago 2006; Salazar-García 2018); Catalan Sign Language (Shaffer et al. 2011); German Sign Language (Pfau & Quer 2007); Irish Sign Language (Herrmann 2008); Russian Sign Language (Borodulina 2012); Italian Sign Language (Gianfreda et al. 2014); Austrian Sign Language (Lackner 2018);

Iranian Sign Language (Siyavoshi 2019); and in Japanese Sign Language and Danish Sign Language (Engberg-Pedersen 2021).

In cognitive and functional studies of signed language modality, two themes that have often been examined are: the possible origin of modal signs from gestures used in the surrounding community, and the grammaticalization of lexical signs to modal signs. Several researchers have suggested that modal signs develop out of gestures commonly used in the surrounding community (Shaffer et al. 2011; Wilcox & Shaffer 2006). These themes overlap: for example, the development of modal signs from gesture suggests that grammaticalization may be at work across these two domains.

A corpus-based study of Brazilian Sign Language (Libras) showed evidence that Libras modals follow similar grammaticization paths that have been reported for spoken languages (Bybee et al. 1994; Auwera & Plungian 1998). The English modal *ought*, for example, indicating general obligation, developed from a lexical word which is now *owe* indicating a specific monetary obligation. Libras PAY (Figure 29) appears to be the lexical source for MUST (Figure 30).

Wilcox (2004) proposed two routes by which gesture may be incorporated into a signed language. The first route begins with a gesture that is not a conventional unit in the relevant sign linguistic system (Figure 31). This gesture becomes incorporated into a signed language as a lexical item. Over time, these lexical signs acquire grammatical function. The second route proceeds along a different path (Figure 32). The source is not a freestanding gesture capable of being incorporated as a lexical item into a signed language. Rather, the source gesture

Figure 29 Libras PAY
(Xavier & Wilcox 2014)

Figure 30 Libras MUST
(Xavier & Wilcox 2014)

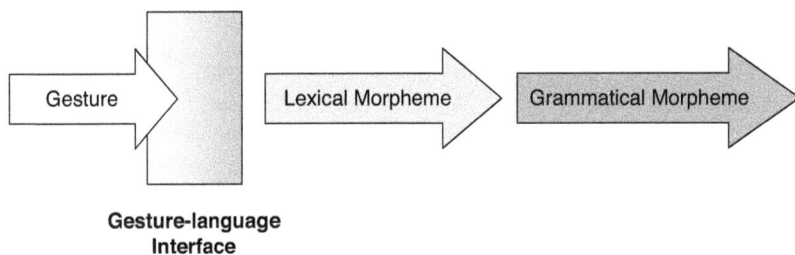

Figure 31 Route 1
(Wilcox 2004 © John Benjamins)

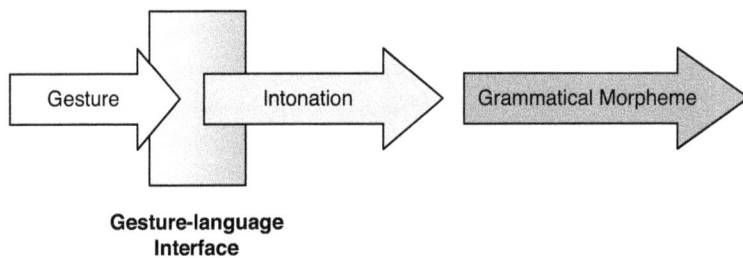

Figure 32 Route 2
(Wilcox 2004 © John Benjamins)

may be one of several types, including a particular manner of movement of a manual gesture or sign – the way in which the gesture or sign is produced – and various facial, mouth, and eye gestures.

One source of evidence for Route 1 comes from the development of the Italian Sign Language (LIS) modal sign meaning it would be *impossible* for something to occur (Figure 33). Wilcox (2009) traces this sign to the "speaking hand" (Barasch 1987), which appeared first in Roman oratory. The gesture was often incorporated into the paintings of Giotto di Bondone, where it was associated with performing a speech act, as in the painting of Saint Francis preaching to the birds (Figure 34) and death, as seen in Giotto's painting of Jesus raising Lazarus from the dead (Figure 35). By this time, the gesture takes on the Roman Catholic meaning of benediction, which incorporates two number metaphors. In the first, the closed fingers (ring and pinky) metaphorically symbolize the two natures of Christ as both human-born and the son of God. In the second, the three extended fingers (thumb, index, and middle) represent the Trinity.

By the early nineteenth century the benediction gesture was commonly associated with death. De Jorio (de Jorio & Kendon 2001, pp. 281–283) describes a gesture he calls "Morte (Death)":

> The sign of the cross is made in the air with an extended hand. This gesture, that is also frequently done with just the index and middle fingers extended, can be used to mean physical death, but it can also refer to moral or political death, since it can be said of someone that he ceases to exist, as far as society is concerned or so far as the estimation of others is concerned.

Figure 33 Italian Sign Language IMPOSSIBLE
(Dizionario Bilingue Elementare della Lingua dei Dei Segni, 175.3)

Figure 34 St. Francis preaching to the Birds (1295–1300)

Finally, the metaphorical extension from physical to moral or political death sanctions a further metonymic link to a meaning of hopelessness and despair (de Jorio & Kendon 2001, p. 283):

> Lost hope, despairing of one's business. It is the same as saying "I am lost, it is finished."

The two-finger gesture drawing a cross in the air and glossed as "dead" is still widely used across Italy by hearing speakers, with the same metaphorical

Figure 35 Jesus raising Lazarus from the dead

extensions noted by De Jorio. Southern Italians (e.g., Neapolitans and Sicilians) also use a variant of this gesture with the same meaning, characterized by a single, continuous circular movement. This variant of the gesture has also been incorporated into LIS to mean "dead" (Figure 36).

Death, whether real or metaphorical, precludes any possible or potential future from coming into existence. This, in turn, leads to hopelessness and despair. The conceptual domain common to both death and despair is *absence of future potential*, and it is this conceptual domain that forms the semantic basis for the modal category of impossibility. In CG, modality is a manifestation of the control cycle and the reality model (Langacker 2013). We have already introduced two types of control: attempting to produce some effect or have influence on the world is effective control, and striving to acquire knowledge of the world is epistemic control. The reality model pertains to how events in the world unfold.

According to the reality model, reality is the history of what has happened up through the present time and is what a conceptualizer conceives as being real or the **reality conception**. Future events are not part of reality because they have not been established. Speakers and signers can, however, make projections of future reality and assess the likelihood of events occurring. Modals express these assessment. For

Figure 36 Italian Sign Language DEAD
(Dizionario Bilingue Elementare della Lingua dei Dei Segni, 175.2)

example, "He will come later" indicates the conceptualizer's assessment that his coming is likely; "He might come later" expresses the conceptualizer's weaker assessment of the likelihood of this future event occurring. Epistemic modals such as IMPOSSIBLE express these epistemic assessments. IMPOSSIBLE expresses the signer's epistemic assessment that the current situation precludes any possible or potential future reality from coming into existence.

In Route 2 the manner of movement of a manual gesture or sign and facial, mouth, and eye gestures are incorporated into a signed language. Here, the route does not proceed to lexical signs but to intonation or prosody, and then to grammatical markers. The dynamics of a sign's movement and certain facial displays have been described as prosody or intonation by a number of researchers (Dachkovsky & Sandler 2009; Nespor & Sandler 1999; Sandler 1999; Wilbur 1990; Wilbur 1999).

Both facial displays and dynamic changes in the movement of signs have been shown to express phonetic stress associated with strength of modal meaning. In Italian Sign Language (LIS), for example, puffed cheeks and various degrees of tense movement, as well as smaller and tighter circular movements of IMPOSSIBLE (Figure 33) are used to express different degrees of epistemic impossibility. These same movement and facial markers appear in ASL and other signed languages to express other grammatical meanings, such as verb aspect and derivation of adjectival predicates (Wilcox, 2004; Wilcox et al. 2010), and strength of deontic and epistemic modality (Wilcox & Wilcox 1995; Wilcox & Shaffer 2006). Frishberg and Gough (Frishberg & Gough 2000) describe a group of ASL signs distinguished by two types of movement they called "sharp" and "soft." Sharp movement is made with single, tense, brisk motion; soft movement is produced with a gentle, repeated, sometimes rocking motion. Signs made with sharp versus soft movement have corresponding meanings. YELLOW produced with sharp movement means "deep yellow"; when made with soft movement the meaning is "light yellow" or "yellowish." These movement distinctions extend to verbal meaning as well. SNOW produced with sharp movement means "blizzard." Signs expressing sudden onset of are made with sharp movement. For example, MEET modified with sharp movement means "bump into" and CRY produced with sharp movement means "burst into tears." Modifications to manner of movement can also apply to movements of the fingers, which Frishberg and Gough call "wiggling" and spritz," where the former is a neutral or canonical movement and the latter is the hand-internal equivalent of sharp. Semantically related wiggling and spritz forms include STUDY and CRAM, AFRAID and TERRIFIED, FIRE/BURN and BURST-INTO-FLAME, and BLEED and BLEED-PROFUSELY.

We would note that these phonological operations on the dynamic qualities of movement are manifestations of baseline and elaboration. The hand is a substantive, baseline structure; its movement (or internal movement of the fingers) is an operation or elaboration yielding a new baseline plus elaboration (BE). This BE is then further elaborated by operations to the dynamic qualities of the movement: smaller, tighter circular movements of IMPOSSIBLE in LIS, sharp/soft and wiggling/spritz movements in ASL.

The grammaticization framework for tracing the gestural sources of signs presented here has also been adopted by other linguists (Janzen & Shaffer 2002; Pfau & Steinbach 2011). In Section 7 we will re-examine the relation between gesture and language. In light of that discussion, we would offer a slightly different account. Rather than seeing the task as one of objectively determining which elements of a usage event are language and which are gesture, we prefer to treat it as a categorization task by a language user.

Determining whether an expression is part of your language or not is a grammaticality judgment. Grammaticality judgments are characterized in cognitive grammar "as categorizing judgments in which the construction in question is characterized as either an instantiation of a particular schema or an extension from that schema" (Van Hoek 1997, p. 44). Deaf language users have developed schemas which serve to categorize usage events. The outcome of this categorization task will depend on the discourse context, the deaf person's prior experience, and the particular deaf person's knowledge, including the person's evolving grammar which provides the set of structures from which one will be selected to categorize the perceived usage event. One implication of this view is that these categories exhibit gradience and dynamic fluidity. This is an approach, we believe, that complements Kusters' notion of a semiotic repertoire, "the totality of semiotic resources that people use when they communicate (such as speech, image, text, gesture, sign, gaze, facial expression, posture, objects and so on)" (Kusters 2021, p. 183). Thus, whereas the previous view was framed in terms of "gesture" becoming "language," this revised view recognizes the active role of the signer in categorizing usage events.

6 The Meaning of Facial Displays

Nonmanual markers or facial displays play an immensely important role in the grammars of signed languages. Lackner (2018, 2019), for example, identifies three major areas – face, mouth, head – capable of articulating more than 100 nonmanual elements expressing such functions as mood and modality, complex propositions (conditionals, causal relations, complementation), information structure (topic, focus), assertions, content and yes/no questions, imperatives, miratives, and more.

Facial displays exhibit two intriguing properties. The same facial display is often associated with different grammatical functions in the same language. A set of facial markers in ASL including raised brow and head tilt may mark conditionals, interrogatives, and topics. These displays also appear in and express similar functions across unrelated signed languages. Zeshan (2004) found in a study of thirty-five geographically and genetically distinct signed languages that all used remarkably similar facial displays, including eyebrow raise, eyes wide open, and eye contact with addressee to mark interrogatives.

Siyavoshi and Wilcox (2021) examined two facial displays: an upper face display called brow furrow in which the eyebrows are pulled tougher, and a lower face display in which the corners of the mouth are turned down into a distinctive configuration that resembles a horseshoe or upside-down U-shape. They propose that these two facial displays manifest two aspects of the control cycle, effective control and epistemic control, and the reality model (Langacker 2013). Effective control describes our striving to influence what happens in the world. Epistemic control consists in constructing and continually updating a conception of reality.

In CG, the reality model captures the idea that the world evolves in a certain way out of all conceivable ways. Reality, according to the model, consists of those events and situations that have occurred up to the present. Epistemic control pertains to our knowledge of reality, our **reality conception**. By contrast, effective control pertains to effecting the course of "real" reality. In CG, the notion of reality is elaborated at multiple levels (Langacker 2013; Langacker 2019). Basic reality pertains to **identification** for objects and **existence** for occurrences: how the profiled thing or occurrence relates to what the interlocutors know. We have shown how identification operates in nominal grounding. For occurrences the epistemic concern is existence – the occurrence's status in relation to reality. A higher level of reality is propositional reality, where the epistemic concern is not whether an event does or does not occur, but the validity of a proposition.

As we have seen in previous sections, the control cycle consists of four phases (Figure 37). Elements of the control cycle include an actor (A), the actor's dominion (D), a field (F), and a target (T). The actor is an entity who strives for control. In the baseline phase, the actor is in a state of stasis or relaxation. In the potential phase some target enters the actor's field, producing a state of tension and requiring the actor to deal with the target in some way. One way of dealing with the tension is an action in which "the actor exerts force in order to capture the target and bring it under control" (Langacker 2013, p. 5).

Effective and epistemic controls are associated with embodied actions which include visually perceptible facial displays. Canonical physical effective control requires effortful activity and the forceful exertion of energy. Physical exertion is commonly correlated with upper face activity, specifically the brow furrow. This display has also been called the "face of effort" and described as "a general converging of the lines to the root of the nose, with transverse wrinkles over the bridge" (McKenzie 1924, pp. 19–20). The brow furrow

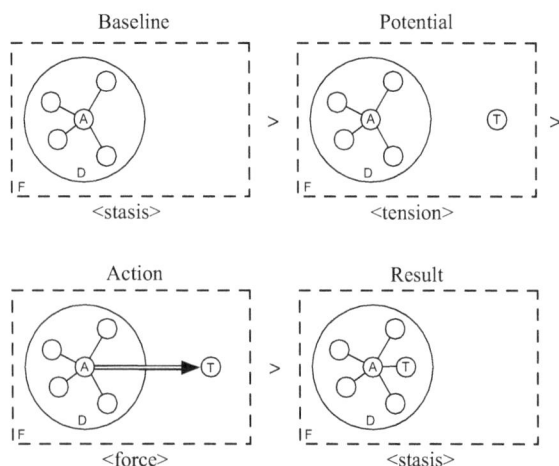

Figure 37 Control cycle
(Langacker 2013)

indicates both physical and mental efforts. The nineteenth-century British anatomist Sir Charles Bell observed that "when the eyebrows are knit, energy of mind is apparent" (Bell 1806, p. 139). Darwin noted that brow furrow marks "the perception of something difficult or disagreeable, either in thought or action" (Darwin 1872, p. 221). The corrugator supercilia facial muscles controlling the brow furrow reflect the degree of physical exertion (de Morree et al. 2010; de Morree & Marcora 2012). Like physical exertion, cognitive effort requires the expenditure of energy, and one correlate of such mental effort is contraction of the corrugator supercilia (Shenhav et al. 2017).

The lower face display or horseshoe mouth is formed by depressing or pulling down the corners of the mouth. This facial display has been attributed such meanings as distancing and disengagement from the world (Streeck 2009), and epistemic indetermination or lessened epistemic endorsement such as ignorance and uncertainty (Debras 2017). According to Chovil (1991), this display suggests a meaning of "I don't know" in the sense of marking epistemic evaluation of an utterance. In infants, the horseshoe mouth has been shown to reflect different states of mind signaling the infant's efforts to control negative emotion and serve a communicative function with caregivers (Camras et al. 2007; Oster et al. 1992). The display has even been observed in ultrasonography of fetuses and identified as an expression of distress (Dondi et al. 2014).

One of the primary goals of communication is to influence our interlocutor – that is, to exert effective control of some type. This may involve directing the attention of the interlocutor in order to achieve intersubjective alignment as seen in nominal grounding, or influencing the interlocutor's knowledge of the world by informing or making an assertion. We may also endeavor to exert effective control by asking a question requiring the interlocutor to produce some utterance, ordering the interlocutor to do something in an imperative, or obligating the interlocutor in some way. Siyavoshi and Wilcox (2021) report that brow furrow is associated with content or wh-questions in at least eleven signed languages, and there are undoubtedly others.

An example of brow furrow accompanying a content question is shown in Figure 38. A Chinese Sign Language native signer has been asked if she will have enough time to go home for Chinese New Year; she asks the interviewer "why" she is asking her such a question. Brow furrow accompanies DOVE "where" (Figure 39) and CHI "who" (Figure 40) in Italian Sign Language.

Brow furrow is also associated with imperatives across a number of unrelated signed languages, including ASL; Argentine Sign Language (Massone & Martinez 2012); Australian Sign Language; Sign Language of the Netherlands (Maier et al. 2013); Iranian Sign Language (Siyavoshi 2019); and others.

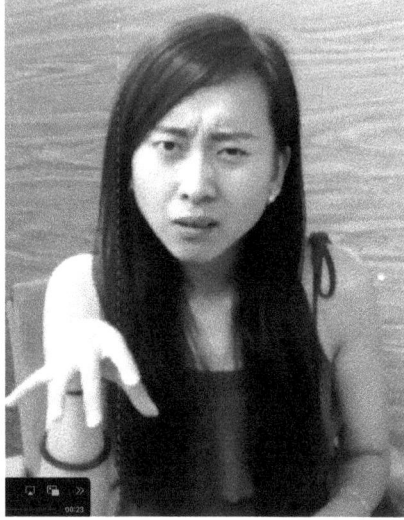

Figure 38 Chinese Sign Language content question
(Saravoshi & Wilcox, 2021)

Figure 39 Italian Sign Language DOVE "where"
(Dizionario Bilingue Elementare della Lingua dei Dei Segni, 594.1)

Another manifestation of effective control is root or deontic modality, typically expressing obligation, permission, or ability. Brow furrow marks necessity,
permission, and obligation in ASL (Shaffer & Janzen 2016; Wilcox & Shaffer
2006). Brow furrow has similar functions in Spanish Sign Language (Iglesias-
Lago 2006) and Brazilian Sign Language (Xavier & Wilcox 2014). In Catalan
Sign Language, deontic modals expressing "must" are accompanied by brow

Figure 40 Italian Sign Language CHI "who"
(Dizionario Bilingue Elementare della Lingua dei Dei Segni, 96.2)

furrow (Shaffer et al. 2011). French Sign Language IL FAUT "must" occurs with brow furrow (Girod 1997). Deontic modality in Italian Sign Language can be accompanied by furrowed eyebrows and/or head nod (Branchini & Mantovan 2020).

In summary, brow furrow is a gradient indicator of exertion. In effective control this exertion is objectively directed at the world, canonically the interlocutor and thus is associated with content questions, orders, and modals expressing obligation. Brow furrow is not, however, associated exclusively with effective control. Brow furrow is an embodied indicator of exertion. In effective control, exertion is aimed at influencing the evolution of reality: the realization of some event – answering a question, performing some action, obligating or otherwise expressing effective modality. Brow furrow may also indicate the exertion of making an epistemic assessment; here where the exertion is aimed at incorporating a proposition into a conception of reality rather than effecting reality. Being a mental activity, the exertion of force in epistemic control is subjective.

Epistemic control is about striving to understand the world rather than influencing what happens in the world. One aspect of epistemic control is the acquisition and control of propositional knowledge. In terms of the control cycle, "At this level, the actor is a conceptualizer, the target is a proposition, and the dominion is the conceptualizer's view of reality (or epistemic dominion), i.e., the set of propositions the conceptualizer currently holds to be valid" (Langacker 2013, p. 131). Examples of epistemic control are making an inference or the use of reasoning to determine some inclination toward accepting or rejecting a conclusion; evaluating the veracity of a memory (e.g., whether some event did or did not occur); and considering or entertaining a possibility. Linguistic expressions of epistemic control include epistemic modality, assertions, and evidentiality.

Expressions of epistemic control are frequently marked with the horseshoe mouth facial display in a number of unrelated signed languages. While horseshoe mouth is not limited to a specific phase of the epistemic control cycle, it often occurs with the potential phase, indicating assessment or inclination. The potential phase can be divided into three stages (Figure 41): formulation, assessment, and inclination (Langacker 2009). In the formulation stage, some proposition (P) enters the conceptualizer's field of awareness. In the assessment stage the conceptualizer actively assesses a proposition to determine its status in relation to the conceptualizer's dominion (D) of established knowledge (the conceptualizer's reality conception). As a result of the assessment, in the inclination stage the conceptualizer arrives at some preliminary judgment regarding the process or proposition (indicated by the double dashed arrow). Langacker (2009, p. 263) observes that although the proposition has a force-dynamic quality at this stage, "in the sense that the status of P vis-à-vis reality is still at issue and has yet to be resolved. Metaphorically, we can think of the inclination stage as a kind of plateau in the climb toward certain knowledge." This force dynamic quality is the exertion required to make a mental assessment, and so we often see horseshoe mouth occur with brow furrow.

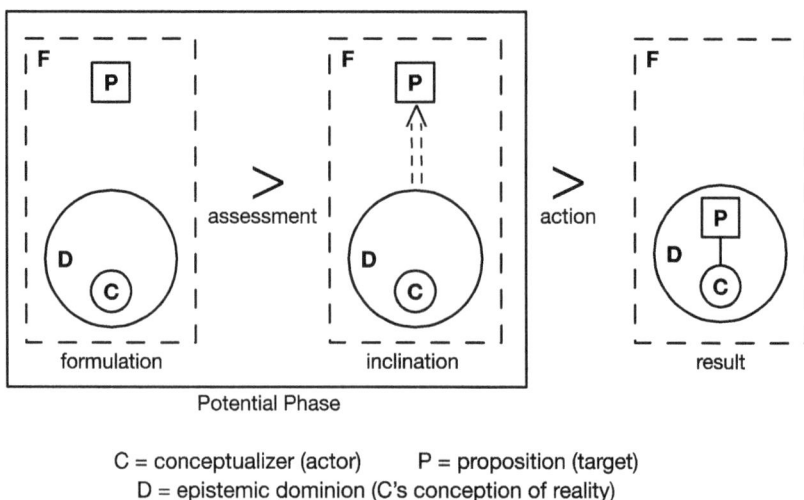

Figure 41 Potential phase stages
(Langacker 2009)

Figure 42 depicts a man describing the age of the boy in a story: "He is five, six, or seven years old . . . five I guess." In terms of the epistemic control cycle, the man has formulated a proposition concerning the boy's age, assessed it, and arrived at an inclination. By signing "five" he indicates that the proposition has been accepted into his epistemic domain (into his reality conception). Squinted eyes and a slight head nod indicate that the validity of the proposition is only weakly accepted. Here we see horseshoe mouth associated with the result phase of the epistemic control cycle.

Epistemic control is also manifested in epistemic modality (Langacker 2013). Epistemic modals also pertain to the potential phase of the epistemic control cycle, specifically expressing various degrees of inclination, such as *may*, *might*, and *must* in English. Horseshoe mouth often accompanies manual signs expressing epistemic modality. In Italian Sign Language, horseshoe mouth and brow furrow are associated with assessments of epistemic certainty/uncertainty, with a meaning such as "I could not confirm with certainty" (Gianfreda et al. 2014). Horseshoe mouth can also mark epistemic possibility. Raised eyebrows and mouth corners down (horseshoe mouth), usually combined with a head tilt backward, express that some event is possible but the signer is not sure due to lack of information (Branchini & Mantovan 2020). In New Zealand Sign Language, modal and epistemic meanings such as uncertainty, doubt, obviousness, and skepticism are marked with horseshoe mouth and raised or furrowed brows co-occurring with palm up (McKee & Wallingford 2011).

Figure 42 Epistemic assessment in Iranian Sign Language
(Siyavoshi & Wilcox 2021)

Horseshoe mouth accompanies lexical signs of epistemic possibility in Spanish Sign Language (Iglesias-Lago 2006) and Iranian Sign Language (Siyavoshi 2019). Possibility and ability are often expressed with the same sign in some signed languages, such as ASL. Typically, ability modals are expressions of effective control. When using a modal to express physical ability, as in "John can lift 500 pounds," the effective force is localized in the subject and directed at the realization of a process by the subject. When the source of effective force is less localizable and more diffuse, the effective meaning of ability modals fades and an epistemic meaning emerges (Langacker 2013). In these cases, ability modals often occur with horseshoe mouth.

In some signed languages, epistemic possibility may be expressed with only the horseshoe mouth. In Spanish Sign Language, for example, Iglesias-Lago (2006, p. 209) reports that "Another face that is used for the expression of the epistemic modality of possibility is the downward movement of the corners of the lips. This, like the arching of the eyebrows, can also function as the sole marker of epistemic modality." Similarly, Italian Sign Language and Iranian Sign Language permit the expression of epistemic modality with only facial displays that include the horseshoe mouth (Branchini & Mantovan 2020; Siyavoshi 2019).

Effective and epistemic controls interact in the exertion required to make an epistemic assessment. They interact in other ways as well. In making an assertion, the signer or speaker believes (or at least presents herself as believing) a proposition and wants to induce the interlocutor to believe it as well. Thus, in an assertion epistemic control is reflected in the assessment of and commitment to the truth of a proposition (Nikolaeva 2016). In terms of the control cycle, "the speaker articulates a proposition that belongs to the speaker's own conception of reality, with the intent of causing the hearer to incorporate that proposition as part of the hearer's conception of reality" (Langacker 2009, p. 158). Assessing and incorporating a proposition is epistemic control. The assertive statement directed at causing the interlocutor to incorporate the proposition constitutes effective control. Assertions are often marked with brow furrow and horseshoe mouth, indicating effective and epistemic control, in a number of signed languages (Siyavoshi & Wilcox 2021).

6.1 From Engaged to Disengaged Cognition

We started this discussion of facial displays by showing that brow furrow and horseshoe mouth are present as behaviors outside of any linguistic system. Brow furrow is associated with physical and mental exertion. The function of horseshoe mouth is less well documented, but it appears to pertain to different states of mind, initially in reaction to the physical environment. In other words, these facial displays originate in our physically embodied interactions with the world – they are physiological responses to the perceptible environment and expressions of the two fundamental imperatives of understanding and controlling the world we inhabit. The restriction that we only have direct access to the world through perceptual and motor systems, and that this experiential interaction is the origin of embodied cognition, were two of our fundamental principles. As described by Langacker (2008, pp. 535–536), "At the most basic level, we interact with the world through our senses and physical actions. There are other levels, of course: much of the world we live in is mentally and socially constructed. But either directly or indirectly, the world we construct and apprehend is grounded in sensory and motor experience."

Direct access to the experiential world is the basis of **engaged cognition**. In effective control we engage the world directly when we use perceptual systems to capture perceptible targets and motor systems to move about and manipulate objects. These activities require actual physical exertion. Similarly, we exhibit epistemic control as we perceive, move around in, and attempt to make sense of the physical world. These interactions with the world require physical and mental effort and are the embodied source of exertion, reflected in brow furrow; striving to make sense of the experienced world – a world that perturbs or disturbs us in ways we attempt to make sense of and control – is the embodied source of horseshoe mouth.

Not all of our experience involves direct engagement with the world. As we develop the world we live in becomes increasingly socially, mentally, and linguistically constructed – disengaged from immediate physical experience. In other words, certain aspects of our cognition are disengaged from the world. Epistemic control is directed at mental constructions – reality conceptions of events in the world, and future or imagined realities.

A significant characteristic of **disengaged cognition** is that it occurs whenever engaged cognition occurs, and it recruits the same neurological and action responses that are present in engaged cognition. In order to understand this relation between engaged and disengaged cognition we must introduce the concept of **subjectification**. As defined in CG, subjectification refers to the process by which "mental operations inherent in experiences of a certain kind are used in abstraction from their content and applied to other circumstances (Langacker 2008, p. 537). An example of subjectification is the mental scanning that occurs in fictive motion (Matlock 2005). In conceptualizing the motion verb *run* when it is used to express an actual motion event, such as "The baseball player ran from first to second base" we use mental scanning to track the motion of the player along a spatial path. In using *run* to express fictive motion, as in "The cut ran from his wrist to his elbow," mental scanning is directed at a static path, building up a holistic conception of the spatial configuration of the cut.

Both of these situations recruit visual perception and motor abilities: the conceptualizer visually tracks the motion of the baseball player, requiring at least a shift in eye gaze and likely movement of the head; these same physical abilities (although perhaps the movements of the eyes and head are attenuated) are used to mentally scan the cut on the man's forearm. As we experience scenes such as this more and more, and in different contexts, we abstract a **scanning scenario** schema (Langacker 2008). The scanning involved in the scanning scenario is now fictive or simulated – no perceptual or motor actions are recruited, and the conceptualization requires only mental scanning. In saying "Basketball players are *usually* tall" the conceptualizer recruits her memory to remember the basketball players from her past experience, mentally scans their height, and sums up over these instances to ascribe the property of being tall as prototypical of the group. In this case, scanning is entirely a cognitive operation: no actual basketball players are visually perceived and no entity moves along a spatial path; the only "path" is the conceptualizer's remembered experiences.

Scanning objective scenes with perceptual and motor abilities to arrive at a conceptualization engages the objective, experiential world. Scanning that is only mental, with attenuated or no direct sensory or motor engagement – as in the scanning operation used to conceptualize fictive motion and the basketball players scanning scenario – is disengaged from the experiential world. Although sensory and motor abilities are not involved, the conceptual operations that are inherent in experiencing the world are recruited, but now they are used in abstraction from any experiential content. This is the disengaged cognition used when saying *usually* to conceptualize an abstract scene.

How does subjectification pertain to engaged and disengaged cognition? Figure 43 (Langacker 2008) shows the relation between engaged and disengaged cognition. In engaged cognition (a), we interact directly with the world

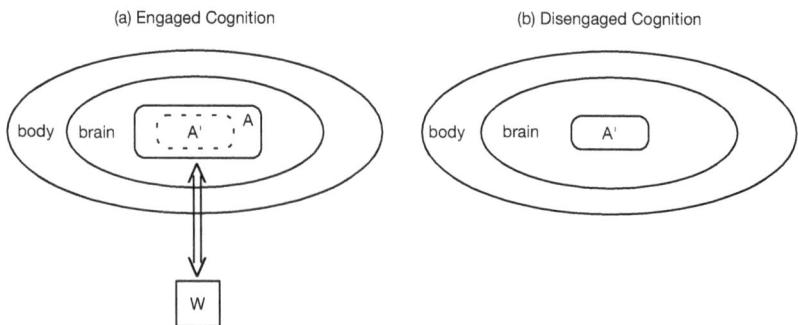

Figure 43 Engaged and disengaged cognition
(Langacker 2008 © Oxford University Press)

(W) by means of embodied perceptual and motor systems (double arrow). Box A represents engaged cognition based on direct physical experience. Diagram (b) depicts disengaged cognition, where certain aspects of engaged cognition (A) are used autonomously (A'), without any direct interaction with the world. These disengaged elements of engaged cognition are **simulations** of A. As we have seen, aspects of cognition that are used without any direct interaction with the world are subjectified: subjectification is one way in which cognition is disengaged from physical, perceptual, motor experience.

Facial displays are transformed from cognitively and experientially engaged to disengaged by subjectification. For brow furrow and exertion, the subjectification of engaged cognition begins in physical activity, where effective control is object-ive, embodied, and requires effort. The cognitive processes required to support such activity are engaged with the world. In linguistic effective control, exertion is still objective, being directed at an interlocutor and aimed at influencing reality. When a signer asks a content question, the interlocutor is expected to produce a response. Here, however, effective control is directed at the social world and not the physical world. No actual physical force is exerted in questions, assertions, or even in ordering someone to do something; the exertion here is simulated. Epistemic control requires effort to be expended, but it is the subjectified mental exertion of disengaged cognition. A similar path can be posited for epistemic control. Here, the baseline level of making sense is contact with the perceptible, physical world. This is engaged experience, and the stage at which horseshoe mouth appears, for example in infants (and even fetuses). Disengaged, linguistic epistemic control is not directed at having an effect on the world, but at creating and updating a conception of the world. It is, we would say, the ongoing process of making sense.

In all the cases of brow furrow and horseshoe mouth discussed here, these facial displays are associated with disengaged cognition and are simulations of their engaged counterparts. While the specific grammatical meanings expressed by these facial displays undoubtedly vary according to the signed language and the constructions in which they appear, the fact that these facial displays express such similar functions across unrelated signed languages is perhaps a reflection of their universal biological heritage that originates in our cognitively engaged, physically embodied interactions with the world.

7 Gesture and Language

7.1 Sign Phonology Redux

We learned in Section 1 that Stokoe's pioneering research set in motion the modern linguistic study of signed languages. His body of work from the late 1950s to the 1990s spanned the history of linguistics from structuralism to the emergence of cognitive linguistics. While cognitive linguistics has now deeply influenced the field of sign linguistics, approaches to sign phonology have remained rooted in structuralism. Structuralist assumptions about the nature of sign phonology have created profound problems for the description and analysis of signed language grammar, raising such issues as the highly iconic nature of signs, the search for signed (visual, optical) equivalents to segments, syllables, prosody and stress, and the relation between phonology and phonetics. The most surprising trend has been the re-emergence of gesture in the description of the grammars of signed languages with the claim that many signs and sign constructions are fusions of language and gesture.

Although Stokoe was not a linguist by training, his academic background, which culminated in a PhD in English specializing in medieval literature, provided him with extensive knowledge of how languages work and how they change. He wrote convincingly, for example, of phonology, morphology, and syntax in Middle English (Stokoe 1955), as well as broader issues of language use, language change, and the interaction of language and culture. Looking back at this experience, he wrote (Stokoe 1994, pp. 377–378):

> My undergraduate and graduate study was focused on language and languages, and at Cornell the study of the classical languages and the tribal languages that became the English language involved also literature – learning about the people who used them and what interested them and what they thought worth writing down. ... Before I came to Gallaudet in 1955 a sabbatical leave from Wells College had enabled me to study carefully what American and European scholars in the developing discipline of linguistics were saying about language and languages. This reading confirmed my belief that when people are interacting with each other constantly, their interaction is nothing other than language, so that the language and their interaction constitute their culture.

When he began teaching deaf students at Gallaudet College, he recognized that their signing was a language. When he was told by his colleagues it was just broken English and gesture he knew something was amiss, and thus started his journey to prove what he already knew: his deaf students were using a language. He turned to the predominant linguists and linguistic theory of the day, studying with linguists George Trager and Henry Lee Smith at the 1957 Summer Institute of Linguistics. Trager and Smith were American structuralists, and thus Stokoe's first analysis was steeped in structuralist linguistic theory.

As we saw in Section 1, Stokoe regarded cheremes as the structural equivalent of phonemes, writing that "Like consonant and vowel," the cheremes of position, configuration, and motion "may only be described in terms of contrast with each other" (Stokoe 2005, p. 20); in other words, the mode of analysis was based on identifying distinctive features. Even at the early stage of his work, however, Stokoe was keenly aware of the important differences between spoken and signed language, especially at the level of phonology. He began to resist the constraints of structuralism and application of theory derived from spoken language. Writing later of this period (Stokoe 1980b), he reported recognizing what he regarded as a central difference: while the phonological elements in spoken languages can only be arranged linearly in the dimension of time (except for stress and intonation), signed languages allow and exploit the three dimensions of space and one of time. His revised thinking on sign structure is worth citing in full (Stokoe 1980b, p. 369):

> In producing a sign language utterance, some part (or parts) of the signer's body acts. If the active part is mobile enough, there are various places in which the action may occur, i.e. begin, take place, or end. But the action, the active part, and the place are all present simultaneously. The problem is to see what composes signs (i.e. what elements they can be decomposed into) when signs are taken as equivalents of words or morphemes of spoken languages. Signs cannot be performed one aspect at a time, as speakers can utter one segment of sound at a time. Signers can of course display handshapes of manual signs ad libitum, but they cannot demonstrate any significant sign action without using something to make that action somewhere. By an act of the imagination, however, it is possible to "look at" a sign as if one could see its action only or its active element only or its location only. In this way *three aspects* of a manual sign of sign language are distinguished, not by segmentation, it must be reemphasized, but by imagination.

By 1980, the influential *The Signs of Language* (Klima & Bellugi 1979) had appeared. The term *parameter* was now being used and understood by most sign linguists as synonymous with Stokoe's term *aspect*. He saw this as a serious error, writing, "More often in recent research the term parameter is used for what is here called an aspect. There is more in this than a quibble over words, which a nonlinguist might suspect" (Stokoe 1980b, p. 371). Stokoe further clarified his view of sign phonology. First, he explained why he considered the switch in terminology from aspects to parameters to be more than a quibble: "My own preference, more philological than linguistic, would be to leave 'parameters' to those who work with quantities and measures generally accepted as quantifiable, and to keep 'aspects' in its literal sense of 'what appears to a specific way of looking'" (Stokoe 1980a, p. 895). A key word here is "quantifiable." In Section 7.2 we will see problems of quantifiability, listability, and countability return. What Stokoe saw as more than a quibble has turned in recent years into a full-fledged disagreement over what distinguishes – and the irony is inescapable – sign from gesture.

Stokoe also observed that another problem arises when the aspect of location is renamed "place of articulation" and considered to be analogous to the concept from spoken language phonetics. Location in signed language, he noted, is not equivalent to place of articulation in speech. The difference is once again because signs occur in visible space. "What is seen is the sign, whereas what the organs of articulation do is shape the sound that is heard. The place or location is always of significance in signing; a sign is where it is" (Stokoe 1980a, p. 896).

Stokoe continued to advance his ideas about sign phonology, moving even farther from structuralism in an article entitled "Semantic Phonology" (Stokoe 1991). Influenced by Wallace Chafe's *Meaning and the Structure of Language* (Chafe 1970), Stokoe reiterated his view that in analyzing the form of a sign, one needs only to think of a sign as something that acts together with its action. From there, he made the conceptual leap of giving meaning to form itself (Stokoe 1991, p. 107):

> I call it semantic phonology. It invites one to look at a sign – i.e. a word of a primary sign language – as simply a marriage of a noun and a verb. In semantic terminology, appropriate here, the sign is an agent-verb construction. The agent is so called because it is what acts (in signing as in generative semantics), and the verb is what the agent does.

In a sense, semantic phonology merely elaborated Stokoe's original vision of sign phonology presented in 1960. The essential idea was there all along: "some thing" that *acts*, and its *action*, the semantic phonological noun and verb. The seed of his aspectual analysis blossomed into what might be seen as the inception of a conceptual approach to sign phonology. Using Cognitive Grammar concepts, we would say that semantic phonology views the thing that acts and its action as conceptual archetypes for prototypical nouns and verbs, as described in Section 3.2. Like prototypical nouns, the acting thing is substantive and conceptually autonomous, residing primarily in space. Its action is conceptually dependent, prototypically energetic, and resides primarily in (change over) time. As an event, action *tout court* is not possible – action requires some thing which performs the action. This means we can also describe semantic phonology in terms of baseline and elaboration. A sign action such as a path movement performs an operation on a more substantive baseline actor, prototypically a hand.

Although Stokoe did not have the conceptual theoretical framework on which to hang his idea of semantic phonology, he did see that it was a new way to view the relation between form and meaning, breaking down the traditional linear view of language where "first there are the sounds (phonology), these are put together to make the words and their classes (morphology), the words in turn, are found to be of various classes, and these are used to form phrase structures (grammar), and finally – the delay is built into this pedestrian way of thinking – the phrase structures after lexical replacement of their symbols yields meaning (semantics)" (Stokoe 1991, p. 112). Instead, he conceived of language in which "semantic phonology ties the last step to the first, making a seamless circuit of this pitty-pat progression. The metaphor for semantic phonology that jumps to mind is the Möbius strip: the input is the output – with a twist!" Stokoe regarded semantic phonology as a more general account for another reason as well: under this conception the actor is not restricted to hands. Facial articulators may equally well serve as actors and their actions: "Semantic phonology admits all kinds and colors of sign activity, welcoming nonmanual as well as manual agents and all their actions" (Stokoe 1991, p. 108). Facial actions such as those we described in Section 6 may also be seen as *operations* on a substantive articulatory base (*raising* eyebrows, *furrowing* the forehead, *lowering* the corners of the mouth, *squinting* the eyes).

In a sense, semantic phonology represented not only the culmination of Stokoe's ongoing journey to move beyond structuralist notions, it also reflected his driving motivation to find simpler solutions. We noted that Stokoe was not initially a linguist. We cannot resist concluding this brief historical sketch with a nod to an article on the topic of Stokoe's original area of expertise, medieval literature. In it, we see a preview of his style of thinking a decade before he became involved in signed languages. Critiquing another scholar's analysis of two sources for the Middle English metrical romance *Sir Launfal*, he wrote, "This theory is not only more complicated than it need be to explain two uncomplicated stories, but it also disparages unjustly the story-telling ability of both the anonymous author and Marie de France" (Stokoe 1948, p. 393). In one succinct sentence Stokoe shows us his preference for simplifying over complicating. Thirty-three years later, in describing semantic phonology, we see the same preference for simplifying: "one needs only to think of a sign as something that acts together with its action; it's that simple: no features, no autosegments, no orientation, no contacting or contacted parts, no HOLDs, no MOVEs, no tiers, no tears – just something acting (limb or limbs, head, face, whatever) along with its action" (Stokoe 1991, pp. 111–112).

In summary, sign phonology began firmly rooted in structuralist thinking. The structuralist approach assumes a universal inventory of phonological elements. Signed language phonological theory adopted these assumptions and searched for a manual phonological inventory of meaningless elements as well. Stokoe's initial analysis and his later dictionary of American Sign Language (Stokoe et al. 1965) did, in fact, offer such an inventory, as have other sign linguists (Liddell & Johnson 1989; Klima & Bellugi 1979). However, decades of phonetic research on spoken language has shown that no inventory of countable phonetic objects exists (Port & Leary 2005). This countable inventory problem is most obvious in attempts to deal with phonological location. Bodily locations – nose, eyes, mouth, hands, fingers – would seem to be tractable problems, easily countable. The problem arises when referents used in grammatical constructions, such as those described in Section 4, occupy spatial locations in the spatiotemporal discourse environment. We discuss the nature of this problem and attempt to resolve it in the next section.

7.2 Location, Location, Location

The historical arc of our understanding of signed languages has taken a surprising trajectory. For centuries signs were regarded as nothing more than holistic, imagistic unanalyzable gesture. With the advent of modern linguistic approaches pioneered by Stokoe, signs were shown to be analyzable based on linguistic principles. Signed languages exhibit the same types of structures – phonological, morphological, syntactic, discourse – as spoken language. Gesture has re-entered the scene in recent years with the claim that signs are composites, or fusions, of language and gesture (Schembri et al. 2018; Meier & Lillo-Martin 2013; Lillo-Martin & Meier 2011). For the reader interested in pursuing the various positions, Wilbur (2013) offers a comprehensive critique from a more formalist perspective. Dotter (2018) gives a detailed and comprehensive summary of the assumptions made by what he calls the "Gesture School" of sign linguistics from a typological and cognitive perspective.

The first step in arguing for signs to be part language and part gesture has been to distinguish the two. A number of criteria have been offered (Brentari 2019; McNeill 1992; McNeill 2000; Sandler 2009), including:

- Gesture lacks hierarchical combinatorial structure
- Gesture is more gradient than language, insofar as the gradience in language is anchored to the language's phonological categories, while gestures are not so constrained.
- Gesture is more variable than language. Sign languages have an established lexicon and morphological categories, while gestures do not.
- Co-speech and co-sign gestures are often produced below the level of aware-ness of speakers and signers, and access implicit, nondeclarative knowledge.
- In language, but not gesture, the phonological and morphological systems distribute their contrasts in a symmetrical fashion within the articulatory and perceptual space using principles of paradigm uniformity

- Gestures are holistic, noncombinatoric, idiosyncratic, and context-sensitive. The linguistic signal is the converse: dually patterned, combinatoric, conventionalized, and far less context-dependent in the relevant sense.

While these criteria may apply to all aspects of sign structure, the predominant current concern focuses on location. Much of the debate questioning whether location is language or gesture has centered around pointing, pronouns, and verb agreement. Liddell (2003) provides an array of examples pointing out the difficulties with specifying locations in pointing constructions (which Liddell calls pointing gestures); reciprocal verbs; indicating verbs (verbs capable of being meaningfully directed in space toward entities, directions, or places); pronouns; and depicting verbs (verbs which include features depicting certain aspects of their meaning). The problem arises because these constructions can use innumerable locations. For example, consider the ASL verb ASK-QUESTION. When a signer asks an addressee a question, ASK-QUESTION is directed at the addressee's chin. The location in three-dimensional space changes when the addressee is much taller than the signer. As Liddell (1990) observes, if the signer imagined facing an exceptionally tall US basketball player, and she wanted to ask him a question, ASK-QUESTION would be directed to a location considerably higher than the signer. Of course, many other factors can determine the location of the addressee. No matter where the addressee is located, ASK-QUESTION is directed at the chin.

Other signs must be directed at other specific parts of the body. GIVE, for example, is directed at the addressee's chest, and COMMUNICATE-TELEPATHICALLY is directed at the addressee's forehead (Liddell 2003). In all of these cases, where the addressee is located, or where a nonpresent addressee is conceptualized as being located, will determine where these signs are directed.

Depicting signs exhibit the same properties. The verb UPRIGHT-PERSON-WALK-ALONG is produced with a path movement. When produced with a particular facial display, the sign means "person walk along in an unhurried movement." As Liddell describes the problem, the sign combines a lexically fixed verb (the index finger symbolizing the upright person) with "variable and gradient initial and final locations" (Liddell 2003, pp. 270–271). As we have seen, Liddell associates these properties with gesture.

Liddell 2003 makes the same case for ASL pronouns. He poses the situation in which a signer is standing on a stage in an auditorium with hundreds of seats, some lower than the stage, some at the level of the stage, and some higher in balconies. In signing YOU to any individual in the auditorium the pronoun has to be directed at the referent, who could be sitting in any of the seats. The direction of pointing – that is, the location of the referent – changes from one referent to the next. Liddell again attributes this to gradience and concludes that these facts about location "are inconsistent with the claim that there is a locus associated with the addressee toward which signs are directed. If there were such a locus, all directional signs referring to the same entity (e.g. the addressee) would be directed toward that single locus" (2003, p. 76). In Liddell's analysis these loci are gradient, variable, uncountable – and thus they are gesture.

But are the different locations toward which signs are directed properly described as gradient? An analogy will provide an answer. Suppose an Olympic archer shoots at a target 50 yards away and 6 feet off the ground. Being a skilled archer, the arrow lands in the center ring of the target. No matter how skilled she is, however, if she continues to shoot arrows at the target they will not land in precisely the same spot. They will disperse in locations around the center ring. This is gradience. The archers aim at one target, but where the multiple shots land will define an area of gradience around the center. If we set up another target and the archer shoots multiple arrows at it, the same will be true. The archer aims at two different locations. Again, multiple hits will define a gradient area around the center. Nevertheless, the archer is shooting at two locations. The fact that there are two locations does not constitute gradience. There is not one immense, gradient target, and the archer does not shoot arrows knowing that she has to hit two targets in order to win, hoping that gradience will direct them to two distinct targets. We can keep adding targets – in fact, there is no necessary end to the number of targets our archer could shoot arrows at. We will get the same result: the number of targets is *not* gradience.

As the analogy pertains to locations in signed languages, the targets are the final locations of the verbs GIVE, ASK-QUESTION, and COMMUNICATE-TELEPATHICALLY. Just as the precise location where multiple arrows aimed at the same target land will exhibit gradience, the signer's index finger in the final location of these verbs will not always hit the same spatial target. But the signer is directing her hand at a specific location: *the addressee's chest, chin,* or *forehead*, no matter where the addressee is or is conceived to be. The central problem is confusing production with conceptualization. Gradience pertains to production. The number and location of real or conceived referents is a matter of conceptualization.

These data presented here pose two theoretical issues, both pertaining to the nature of grammar and to sign phonology: (1) the number of possible locations, and (2) how the connection between a referent and its phonological location is specified. Both issues arise because of how sign linguistics approaches phonology. For many sign linguists, phonology assumes a list – a finite inventory of distinctive phonemes. The inability to list every possible phonological location leads sign linguists to claim that these locations cannot be part of a grammatical system, and therefore they must be gesture. Liddell recognizes the need to specify phonological locations, but we saw he attributes these specifications to gradience and thus gesture: "Each individual verb has specific gestural characteristics associated with it" (2003, p. 139). Wilbur (2013, pp. 222–223), although she does not accept this argument, summarizes it succinctly with regard to the first problem:

> Liddell (2003, 2011) has argued that since directional verbs move between spatial locations associated with referents, and since there are an infinite number of possible points, the forms of these verbs are unlistable, and are therefore just gestural indications of the referent ... Thus, the argument goes, if the locations in space that are used for indexic and referential pointing are not listable, they cannot be part of the grammar, and therefore must be external to it, that is, part of "gesture".

The ramifications are profound because constructions of the type under discussion are pervasive in signed languages. By this reasoning, these types of constructions must be fusions of gestural locations and linguistic elements (Schembri et al. 2018), or blends "in which gestural and linguistic elements are co-produced within a single sign" (Özyürek 2012, p. 637).

Concerning the second theoretical issue, Lillo-Martin and Meier (2011, p. 121) adopt a theory in which "actual real-world locations of referents are not part of the grammar, so in order for a linguistic object to 'point to' such locations, language must interface closely with the gestural system." In Lillo-Martin and Meier's approach, abstract indices are defined in the grammar, whereas real-world loci are outside of grammar. This constrains how they can explain the connection between a referent and its location. As a result, they conclude that "the grammar doesn't care which point in space is used for a particular referent ... the connection between referents and loci requires language to interface with gesture" (Lillo-Martin & Meier 2011, p. 121). Liddell relates this problem to phonology, saying that "describing a spatial locus in terms of some type of phonological or phonetic feature has proven to be extremely difficult and there is currently no satisfactory feature system capable of doing this" (Liddell 2003, p. 136).

Such theoretical approaches lead to the untenable position that a core element of signed languages is gesture. The grammar of a signed language is incapable of telling signers how to point to a real-world location, such as a cup of cappuccino, and say "This is the best cappuccino I've ever had." Surprisingly, gesture is able to do all of this quite well, so well that even a child can do it. One might ask: how is gesture able to do what grammar cannot? Does gesture keep a list of all the locations that a person can point to? Does gesture keep a list of all the locations of addressee's chins, whether the addressee was taller or shorter than the signer, lying on the floor, standing on the roof, or rising aloft in a hot air balloon? We suspect that is not how gesture handles what grammar cannot. But the suggestion that grammar has to interface with gesture clearly recognizes that a solution to the problem does exist – it's just that this approach to grammar cannot solve it, and so the problem is handed off to gesture. We might ask why, once we understand how gesture handles the problem, grammar could not use the same solution, unless linguists have so handcuffed grammar that we are left to grasp at straws in order to conform to self-imposed theoretical constraints.

Traditional linguistic theory presupposes that semantics and phonology – the meaningful and the meaningless – are independent domains of language. As a result of this disjunction, the ability of the grammar to connect referents with their locations breaks down and the problem must be turned over to gesture. It should come as no surprise that we do not accept a view of language that requires two distinct fields of cognitive potential and an interface between the two. When a signer places and points to two locations on her left and right to compare two abstract ideas, perhaps pilot wave theory and many-worlds theory alternatives to the Copenhagen interpretation of quantum mechanics; when a signer directs signs at a location on her left when telling a story about a conversation with an imaginary Golden Hand man; when a signer points to the former location of a building that was torn down and is no longer there; when a mother directs the sign FINISH at a lower location when telling her deaf son to stop misbehaving; when a young deaf boy directs the ASL sign ASK upward when talking to his favorite basketball player; when a signer points to and directs her eye gaze at the addressee standing in front of her; when a signer points to the location of an absent cappuccino cup that only a few seconds previously was on the table and asks where it went; when a signer points to her iPhone and signs, "that's my iPhone"; when a signer points to her nose to mean "nose" – all of these usage events make use of *symbolic structures*, an association of a semantic pole and a phonological pole, symbolic structures that we have analyzed as Places. In all cases, the conceptualized location of an entity is symbolically realized as an actual phonological location. We see no reason why some of these locations should be accepted as linguistic and others denied linguistic citizenship.

Places are symbolic structures consisting of a schematic semantic pole ("thing") and a schematic phonological pole (a location in space). Through our experience with the world we construct intersecting hierarchical networks of Places with varying degrees of semantic and phonological schematicity/ specificity. Cognitive abilities such as memory and imagination operate to yield other types of Places, with increased detachment from perception of the experiential world requiring increased conceptual resources. By using these general cognitive abilities and the linguistic resource of Places, signers are able to instantiate and direct attention to an unlimited number of Places that refer to distinct discourse entities.

This approach may not seem like the type of simple, parsimonious model of grammar that a linguist should propose – better to deport the uncountable offending elements. Our reply would be, "we judge theories not by the number of entities they can and do describe but by the simplicity of their underlying ideas."[9] Our approach has a single underlying idea. Our account is grounded in established Cognitive Grammar and does not postulate new theoretical con-structs. Places are simply symbolic structures that exploit space for their phonological expression. Yes, we posit a conceptual network of Places, and we recruit cognitive abilities. But linguistic theories already have semantic and phonological networks, and the cognitive abilities are already well established, for both linguistic and nonlinguistic conceptualization. On the other hand, approaches that require the most common elements of signed language expres-sions to be fusions of two distinct systems, and suggest that knowing how to point to and talk about an object in the environment requires a system distinct from language, with the additional complication of an interface between the two – these approaches seem not so simple.

Liddell (2003) develops an extensive cognitive account of ASL grammar based on mental space and blending theory (Fauconnier 1985; Fauconnier 1997; Fauconnier & Turner 1996). Mental space theory is based on cognitive linguis-tic principles, including the experiential grounding of language and cognition in human's perceptual-motor interaction with the spatial environment. And yet, Liddell's model imposes the structural barrier between phonological space and semantic space that forces him to classify certain locations as gestural. His 2003 account holds to the assumption that ASL "consists of more than conventional linguistic forms. It also includes gradient aspects of the signal (typically direc-tional aspects or placement) and gestures of various types." As a result, Liddell believed that "ignoring gestures and gradient aspects of the signal produced by the hands leaves out too much" and that "restricting the analysis of language to symbolic units and their grammatical organization is hopelessly inadequate" (2003, p. 362). The problem is these are not gradient, nonconventional, non-symbolic aspects of ASL. Constructions that incorporate the spatial locations

---

[9] This is not actually our reply. We took it from Sean Carroll, a theoretical physicist from the California Institute of Technology and the Santa Fe Institute, from his book *Something Deeply Hidden: Quantum Worlds and the Emergence of Spacetime* (2019), page 153, in which he describes the many-worlds theory of quantum mechanics.

necessarily used in pointing, placing, and multiple symbolization are fully analyzable as conventional, symbolic linguistic units.

Finally, we should note that in their latest work, Johnson and Liddell (2019, 2021) do not use the term gesture. Rather, they propose a phonetic system based on placement bearings – the term "bearing" borrowed from its navigational meaning – which describe the direction a hand points. They also divide signed languages into two broad categories of signs: indicating signs (agreement, directional, etc.) such as SAY-NO-TO→y and ASK-QUESTION, and nonindicating signs such as MOTHER, EAT, TREE, LIKE.

The clash of a cognitive linguistic approach to the grammar of signed languages as developed by Liddell and a lingering structural approach to sign phonology plays out in this proposed phonetic system. In indicating signs, the bearings are "ad hoc pointing directions the signer must conceptualize and receivers must construct in their own minds" (Liddell & Johnson 2019, p. 167). In contrast, nonindicating signs require a "phonetic inventory of lexically fixed bearings." These two contrasting requirements derive from the same problem caused by the uncountable spatial locations of referents, particularly in indicating signs. As we have seen, these spatial locations were branded as gesture and excluded from the linguistic system. The current proposal is simply silent on spatial locations: "spatial loci no longer play a role in our phonetic representations of hand placement" (ibid., p. 167).

Navigational systems certainly work. Clearly, however, navigational systems imply a destination: in a nautical navigational system the destination is the spatial location toward which the ship sails. Ships do not set a bearing simply for the sake of setting a bearing. The raison d'être of the bearing is to reach the destination. For signers, the sole purpose of a hand placement bearing for indicating signs is to identify for the interlocutor a referent occupying a particular location in space. Johnson and Liddell acknowledge, as they must, not only that the spatial locations are the destinations of the hand bearing, but that they remain (at least in their view) uncountable: "indicating signs require a different conception of phonetics, one that includes nonlistable phonetic features (i.e., placement bearings and displacement bearings that point at people and things)" (ibid., p. 167).

The move to a hand placement bearing approach strikes us as sleight-of-hand, and yet another complication imposed by structuralist thinking: rather than admitting spatial locations into the grammar of language and describing them directly, the proposed model describes the bearings that indirectly point to entities which signers know to occupy spatial locations. As Johnson and Liddell state (ibid., p. 145): "It is important to note that we are proposing an uncountable number of ways an indicating verb can point, not an uncountable number of meaningful spatial loci or an uncountable number of grammatical elements."

Signed languages use space. Signers use locations in space for the purpose of constructing meaning. If existing linguistic theories cannot account for such things, then surely this is too bad for linguistic theories. Turn the page and start rethinking. Our proposal, we believe, is at once simpler and targets what the signer is actually conceptualizing. Meaningful spatial locations are elements of the expression of signed languages – they are the phonological pole of Place symbolic structures. This proposal does not require an uncountable number of grammatical elements. It needs only one, the grammatical element of Place, a schematic symbolic structure which, like the grammatical element *noun*, has uncountable instantiations.

Cognitive Grammar holds that phonological space is a subregion of semantic space, and thus a linguistic symbol is "a correspondence between two structures in semantic space (broadly conceived) where one occupies the phonological subregion" (Langacker 1987, p. 79). In other words, phonological structures are conceptual. The phonological location of Place is a conceptual entity. How phonological entities are realized phonetically certainly requires explication. We believe the best solution will lie in task dynamic approaches such as has been applied to speech and to motor action (Browman & Goldstein 2010b; Hawkins 1992; Saltzman & Kelso 2009; Thelen & Smith 1994). One such model is articulatory phonology (Browman & Goldstein 1990; Browman & Goldstein 2010a). Application of such models to signed language would seem a natural extension, but little work has been done toward making the connection (see, however, Tyrone et al. 2010 and Silva & Xavier 2018).

7.3 Science or Ethnoscience?

This leaves us with the question: what is gesture? The urge to distinguish between language and gesture is ancient. For most of this time the distinction appeared simple and natural: language is speech, gesture is predominantly what the hands do, including signing. This simple solution of equating language with speech and gesture with the hands does not work in the face of signed languages. As we have just seen, sign linguists began to look for approaches to distinguish language and gesture based on more refined criteria; some called for defining a modality free notion of gesture (Okrent 2002), with little substance on what such a notion would entail.

We question whether objective criteria can ever be specified that will uniquely distinguish "language" from "gesture." In light of what we now know about signed languages and the multimodality of communicative behavior, we question whether "gesture" is even a useful scientific concept. Adam Kendon, one of the most distinguished scholars working on gesture today, raises the same question:

> "Gesture" is so muddied with ambiguity, and theoretical and ideological baggage, that its use in scientific discourse impedes our ability to think clearly about how kinesic resources are used in utterance production and interferes with clarity when comparing signers and speakers. (Kendon 2017, p. 30)

Kendon argues that it is time to discard the categories "gesture" and "sign" and develop a comparative semiotics of visible bodily action (kinesis) used in utterances by speakers and by signers. He suggests that doing so would "resolve and clarify the otherwise rather fraught discussions of how 'gesture' and sign' are related, as well as the problems encountered when, in a signed utterance, we sometimes have difficulty in deciding whether a given expression is a 'gesture' or a 'sign'" (Kendon 2017, p. 30).

We use "perceptible usage events" as a term that includes bodily actions that are visually perceived as well as bodily actions that produce an acoustic signal that is perceived by the auditory system. These are the same bodily actions that, as we discussed in Section 2, Neisser (1967) calls articulatory gestures, and the gestural units of articulatory phonology described at the end of the previous section. In this sense, spoken language, signed language, and gesture are all gestural. As we have noted, perceptible events do not come to language users as sorted, listed, and labeled phenomena. The search for categorical, objective, observable criteria that will distinguish between language and gesture seems to us the wrong approach. "Language" and "gesture" are not, we submit, scientific concepts. They are ethnoscientific concepts.

We are reminded of two stories told by cultural anthropologists. The first is from William Sturtevant (1964, p. 100), who defines culture as

> the sum of a given society's folk classifications, all of that society's ethnoscience, its particular ways of classifying its material and social universe. Thus, to take an extreme example, the "ethnopornography" of the Queensland aborigines is what they consider pornographic – if indeed they have such a category – rather than what was considered pornography by the Victorian ethnologist [who studied them].

The second story comes from the cultural anthropologist Clifford Geertz (1973, p. 6):

> Consider two boys rapidly contracting the eyelids of their right eyes. In one, this is an involuntary twitch; in the other, a conspiratorial signal to a friend. The two movements are, as movements, identical; from an I-am-a-camera "phenomenalistic" observation of them alone, one could not tell which was twitch and which was wink, or indeed whether both or either was twitch or wink. Yet

the difference, however unphotographable, between a twitch and a wink is vast; as anyone unfortunate enough to have had the first taken for the second knows. As Ryle points out, the winker has not done two things, contracted his eyelids and winked, while the twitcher has done only one, contracted his eyelids. Contracting your eyelids on purpose when there exists a public code in which so doing counts as a conspiratorial signal is winking. That's all there is to it: a speck of behavior, a fleck of culture, and – voilà! – a gesture.

The answer to figuring out what is what lies with the observer, not the observed. As early as 1960, Stokoe recognized that sign linguists should not impose criteria to distinguish sign from gesture; rather, they should see the world as a deaf person would. As he wrote (Stokoe 1960, pp. 6–7):

> To take a hypothetical example, a shoulder shrug, which for most speakers accompanied a certain vocal utterance, might be a movement so slight as to be outside the awareness of most speakers; but to the deaf person, the shrug is unaccompanied by anything perceptible except a predictable set of circumstances and responses; in short, it has a definite "meaning".

Stokoe's shrug, Ryle's wink, and the other perceptible events deaf people experience every moment of their life is the stuff from which language is made. The same behavior, with a different fleck of experience and a speck of categorization by the observer, and – voilà! – language. The answer to Kendon's question of whether a given expression is a "gesture" or a "sign," or to whether certain expressions are language-gesture fusions or not, lies not in finding observable, linguist-as-a-camera photographable differences between "sign" and "gesture." It is a matter of what counts as sign or gesture from the observer's point of view. This, in turn, depends on received folk classifications that are handed down and change over time, that vary across cultures and across the individuals doing the classification. "Language," "gesture," and "sign" are historical-cultural constructs, folk classifications. Whether deaf and hearing people, not to mention regular folk and linguists, share the same classifications of what counts as sign and what counts as gesture – if indeed communities of signed language users even have such categories – is an open and important question. Research suggests that the answer is likely to be quite complex (Kusters & Sahasrabudhe 2018).

8 Conclusions

Our Element's contribution on signed languages and Cognitive Grammar had three primary objectives. First, we aimed to provide sign linguists with a comprehensive understanding of the fundamental principles of Cognitive Grammar. We believe this framework whose basic assumptions – different, and, at moments, at odds with more dominant formal assumptions within the linguistic field – has a great potential for analyzing not only well described spoken languages such as English or Spanish, but also understudied, minority languages, as is the case of the hundreds of signed languages in the world. By examining a range of grammatical phenomena in different signed languages within Cognitive Grammar (nominal grounding, antecedent-anaphor constructions, referent tracking, role shift, modality, and others), we hope to encourage further exploration of this theoretical framework.

Second, we sought to familiarize readers, particularly those with a background in the broader area of cognitive linguistics but limited exposure to signed language data, with the unique linguistic phenomena and challenges encountered by signed language linguists. By presenting examples of these distinctive challenges, such as the problems posed by clear-cut definitions of gesture in the context of analyzing signed languages, we aimed to broaden the perspective of scholars within the linguistic field, fostering a deeper understanding of the complexities involved in the study of signed languages.

Finally, our contribution addressed the need for a fresh approach in studying signed language linguistics. Historically, signed language linguists often relied on theories developed to explain the structure of spoken languages and sought analogies in signed languages. Even though these analyses and decisions were relevant to the pursuit of validating signed languages as natural languages that have the same status of spoken languages, we believe it is now time to pursue the study of signed languages through different theoretical lenses that acknowledge their unique properties and distinctiveness from spoken languages. While recognizing that signed languages are indeed human languages and that connections with spoken languages may emerge, we emphasized the importance of understanding these connections within the framework of shared conceptual abilities rooted in embodied sensorimotor experiences.

References

Auwera, Johann van der & Vladimir A. Plungian. 1998. Modality's semantic map. *Linguistic Typology*, *2*, 79–124.

Bakhtin, Mikhail Mikhaïlovich. 1981. *The dialogic imagination: Four essays.* Austin, TX: University of Texas Press.

Barasch, Moshe. 1987. *Giotto and the language of gesture.* Cambridge: Cambridge University Press.

Barlow, Michael. 1999. Agreement as a discourse phenomenon. *Folia Linguistica*, *33*(1–2), 187–210.

Battison, Robbin. 1978. *Lexical borrowing in American Sign Language.* Silver Spring, MD: Linkstok Press.

Bell, Charles. 1806. *Essays on the anatomy of expression in painting.* London: Longman.

Borodulina, Darija. 2012. Means of expressing the possibility and necessity in Russian Sign Language. *Bulletin of Tomsk State Pedagogical University, 1*, 92–95.

Branchini, Chiara & Lara Mantovan (eds.). 2020. *A grammar of Italian Sign Language (LIS).* Venice: Edizioni Ca'Foscari.

Brentari, Diane. 2007. Sign language phonology: Issues of iconicity and universality. *Empirical Approaches to Language Typology*, *36*, 59–80.

Brentari, Diane. 2019. *Sign language phonology.* Cambridge: Cambridge University Press.

Brito, Lucinda Ferreira. 1990. Epistemic, alethic, and deontic modalities in a Brazilian Sign Language. In Susan D. Fischer & Patricia Siple (eds.), *Theoretical issues in sign language research Vol. 1: Linguistics* (pp. 229–260). Chicago, IL: University of Chicago Press.

Browman, Catherine P. & Louis M. Goldstein. 1990. Gestural specification using dynamically-defined articulatory structures. *Journal of Phonetics*, *18*, 299–320.

Browman, Catherine P. & Louis M. Goldstein. 2010a. Articulatory gestures as phonological units. *Phonology*, *6*, 201–251.

Browman, Catherine P. & Louis M. Goldstein. 2010b. Towards an articulatory phonology. *Phonology yearbook*, *3*, 219–252.

Bybee, Joan, Revere Perkins, & William Pagliuca. 1994. *The evolution of grammar: Tense, aspect, and modality in the languages of the world.* Chicago, IL: University of Chicago Press.

Cabeza-Pereiro, Carmen. 2013. Modality and linguistic change in Spanish Sign Language (LSE): Obligation and epistemic necessity from the Fernández Villabrille dictionary (1851) to the DNLSE (2008). *CogniTextes: Revue de l'Association française de linguistique cognitive, 10,* 1–16.

Camras, Linda A., Harriet Oster, Roger Bakeman, et al. 2007. Do infants show distinct negative facial expressions for fear and anger? Emotional expression in 11-month-old European American, Chinese, and Japanese infants. *Infancy, 11*(2), 131–155.

Chafe, Wallace. 1970. *Meaning and the structure of language.* Chicago, IL: University of Chicago Press.

Chafe, Wallace. 1982. Integration and involvement in speaking, writing, and oral literature. In Deborah Tannen (ed.), *Spoken and written language: Exploring orality and literacy* (pp. 35–53). Norwood, NJ: Ablex.

Chafe, Wallace. 1994. *Discourse, consciousness, and time: The flow and displacement of conscious experience in speaking and writing.* Chicago: University of Chicago Press.

Chovil, Nicole. 1991. Discourse-oriented facial displays in conversation. *Research on Language & Social Interaction, 25*(1–4), 163–194.

Clark, Herbert H. 2003. Pointing and placing. In Satoro Kita (ed.), *Pointing: Where language, culture, and cognition meet* (pp. 243–268). Mahwah, NJ: Psychology Press. http://web.stanford.edu/~clark/2000s/Clark,H.H._Pointingand pla cing_2003.pdf.

Cormier, Kearsy, Sandra Smith, & Martine Zwets. 2013. Framing constructed action in British Sign Language narratives. *Journal of Pragmatics, 55,* 119–139.

Croft, William. 2001. *Radical construction grammar: Syntactic theory in typological perspective.* Oxford: Oxford University Press.

Croft, William. 2013. Agreement as anaphora, anaphora as coreference. In Dik Bakker & Martin Haspelmath (eds.), *Languages across boundaries: Studies in memory of Anna Siewierska* (pp. 107–129). Berlin: De Gruyter.

Cysouw, Michael. 2011. Very atypical agreement indeed. *Theoretical Linguistics,* 153–160.

Dachkovsky, Svetlana & Wendy Sandler. 2009. Visual intonation in the prosody of a sign language. *Language and Speech, 37*(52), 287–314.

Darwin, Charles. 1872. *The expression of the emotions in man and animals.* London: J. Murray.

de Jorio, Andrea & Adam Kendon. 2001. *Gesture in Naples and gesture in classical antiquity: A translation of La mimica degli antichi investigata nel gestire napoletano, Gestural expression of the ancients in the light of Neapolitan gesturing.* Bloomington, IN: Indiana University Press.

de Morree, Helma M. & Samuele M. Marcora. 2010. The face of effort: Frowning muscle activity reflects effort during a physical task. *Biological Psychology*, *85*(3), 377–382.

de Morree, Helma M. & Samuele M. Marcora. 2012. Frowning muscle activity and perception of effort during constant-workload cycling. *European Journal of Applied Physiology*, *112*(5), 1967–1972.

Debras, Camille. 2017. The shrug: Forms and meanings of a compound enactment. *Gesture*, *16*(1), 1–34.

Dondi, Marco, Maria Teresa Gervasi, Angela Valente, et al. 2014. Spontaneous facial expressions of distress in fetuses. In Cristina De Sousa & Armando M. Oliviera (eds.), *Proceedings of the 14th European Conference on Facial Expression* (pp. 34–37). Coimbra: IPCDVS. www.researchgate.net/profile/ Marco_Dondi/publication/262727826_Spontaneous_Facial_Expressions_ of_Distress_in_Fetuses/links/563dc5b208ae8d65c012a30d/Spontaneous-Facial-Expressions-of-Distress-in-Fetuses.pdf.

Dotter, Franz. 2018. Most characteristic elements of sign language texts are intricate mixtures of linguistic and non-linguistic parts, aren't they? *Colloquium: New Philologies*, *3*(1), 1–62.

Dudis, Paul G. 2004. Body partitioning and real-space blends. *Cognitive Linguistics*, *15*, 223–238.

Edelman, Gerald M. 1987. *Neural Darwinism: The theory of neuronal group selection*. New York: Basic Books.

Emmorey, Karen. 2014. Iconicity as structure mapping. *Philosophical Transactions of the Royal Society of London. Series B, Biological Sciences*, *369*.

Engberg-Pedersen, Elisabeth. 1993. *Space in Danish Sign Language: The semantics and morphosyntax of the use of space in a visual language*. Hamburg: SIGNUM-Verlag.

Engberg-Pedersen, Elisabeth. 1999. Space and time. In Jens Allwood & Peter Gärdenfors (eds.), *Cognitive semantics: Meaning and cognition* (pp. 131–152). Amsterdam: John Benjamins.

Engberg-Pedersen, Elisabeth. 2015. Perspective in signed discourse: The privileged status of the signer's locus and gaze. *Open Linguistics*, *1*, 411–431.

Engberg-Pedersen, Elisabeth. 2021. Markers of epistemic modality and their origins: Evidence from two unrelated sign languages. *Studies in Language*, *45*(2), 277–320.

Fauconnier, Gilles. 1985. *Mental spaces*. Cambridge, MA: MIT Press.

Fauconnier, Gilles. 1997. *Mappings in thought and language*. New York: Cambridge University Press.

Fauconnier, Gilles & Mark Turner. 1996. Blending as a central process of grammar. In Adele E. Goldberg (ed.), *Conceptual structure, discourse, and language* (pp. 113–130). Stanford, CA: Center for the Study of Language and Information Publications.

Ferrara, Lindsay & Trevor Johnston. 2014. Elaborating who's what: A study of constructed action and clause structure in Auslan (Australian Sign Language). *Australian Journal of Linguistics*, *34*, 193–215.

Fischer, Susan & Bonnie Gough. 1978. Verbs in American Sign Language. *Sign Language Studies*, *18*(1), 17–48.

Fowler, Carol A. 2010. Embodied, embedded language use. *Ecological Psychology*, *22*, 286–303.

Frishberg, Nancy. 1975. Arbitrariness and iconicity: Historical change in American Sign Language. *Language: Journal of the Linguistic Society of America*, *51*, 676–710.

Frishberg, Nancy & Bonnie Gough. 2000. Morphology in American Sign Language. *Sign Language & Linguistics*, *3*, 103–131.

Geertz, Clifford. 1973. *The interpretation of cultures*. New York: Basic Books.

Gianfreda, Gabriele, Virginia Volterra, & Andrzej Zuczkowski. 2014. L'espressione dell'incertezza nella Lingua dei Segni Italiana (LIS). *Ricerche di Pedagogia e Didattica. Journal of Theories and Research in Education*, *9*(1), 199–234.

Girod, Michel. 1997. *La langue des signes: Tome 1, 2, and 3. Dictionnaire bilingue elementaire*. Vincennes: International Visual Theatre.

Goodale, Melvyn A. 1998. Vision for perception and vision for action in the primate brain. *Novartis Foundation Symposium*, *218*, 21–34.

Grice, Paul. 1989. *Studies in the way of words*. Cambridge, MA: Harvard University Press.

Hawkins, Sarah. 1992. An introduction to task dynamics. In Gerard L. Docherty & D. Robert Ladd (eds.), *Papers in laboratory phonology II: Gesture, segment, prosody* (pp. 9–25). Cambridge: Cambridge University Press.

Herrero-Blanco, Ángel & Ventura Salazar-García. 2010. The expression of modality in Spanish Sign Language. *Web Papers in Functional Discourse Grammar (WP-FDG)*, 19–42.

Herrmann, Annika. 2008. The expression of modal meaning in German Sign Language and Irish Sign Language. In Pamela M. Perniss, Roland Pfau, & Markus Steinbach (eds.), *Visible Variation: Comparative Studies on Sign Language Structure* (pp. 245–278). Berlin: Mouton de Gruyter.

Hockett, Charles F. 1982. The origin of speech. In William S.-Y. Wang (ed.), *Human communication: Language and its psychobiological bases* (pp. 5–12). San Francisco, CA: W. H. Freeman.

Iglesias-Lago, Silvia. (2006). *Uso del componente facial para la expresión de la modalidad en lengua de signos española*. Ph.D. Universidade de Vigo, Vigo, Spain.

Janzen, Terry. 2006. Visual communication: Signed language and cognition. In Gitte Kristiansen, Michel Achard, René Dirven, & Francisco Ruiz Mendoza de Ibáñez (eds.), *Cognitive linguistics: Current applications and future perspectives* (pp. 359–377). Berlin: Mouton de Gruyter.

Janzen, Terry. 2012. Lexicalization and grammaticalization. In Martin Steinbach, Roland Pfau, & Bencie Woll (eds.), *Handbook of Sign Languages (34)* (pp. 816–840). Berlin: Mouton de Gruyter.

Janzen, Terry, Barbara O'Dea, & Barbara Shaffer. 2001. The construal of events: Passives in American Sign Language. *Sign Language Studies, 1*, 281–310.

Janzen, Terry & Barbara Shaffer. 2002. Gesture as the substrate in the process of ASL grammaticization. In Richard Meier, David Quinto, & Kearsy Cormier (eds.), *Modality and structure in signed and spoken languages* (pp. 199–223). Cambridge: Cambridge University Press.

Jarque, Maria Josep & Esther Pascual. 2015. Direct discourse expressing evidential values in Catalan Sign Language. *eHumanista/IVITRA, 8*, 421–445.

Jarque, Maria Josep & Esther Pascual. 2016. Mixed viewpoints in factive and fictive discourse in Catalan Sign Language narratives. In Barbara Dancygier, Wei-lun Lu, & Arie Verhagen (eds.), *Viewpoint and the fabric of meaning: Form and use of viewpoint tools across languages and modalities* (pp. 259–280). Berlin: Mouton de Gruyter.

John-Steiner, Vera. 1997. *Notebooks of the mind: Explorations of thinking.* Oxford: Oxford University Press.

Johnson, Mark. 1987. *The body in the mind: The bodily basis of meaning, imagination, and reason.* Chicago, IL: University of Chicago Press.

Johnson, Robert E. & Scott K. Liddell. 2021. Toward a phonetic description of hand placement on bearings. *Sign Language Studies, 22*(1), 131–180.

Johnston, Trevor & Adam Schembri. 2007. *Australian Sign Language (Auslan): An introduction to sign language linguistics.* Cambridge: Cambridge University Press.

Kendon, Adam. 2017. Languages as semiotically heterogenous systems. *Behavioral and Brain Sciences, 40*, 30–31.

Kibrik, Andrej A. 2019. Rethinking agreement: Cognition-to-form mapping. *Cognitive Linguistics, 30*(1), 37–83.

Klima, Edward & Ursula Bellugi. 1979. *The signs of language.* Cambridge, MA: Harvard University Press.

Kusters, Annelies. 2021. Introduction: The semiotic repertoire: Assemblages and evaluation of resources. *International Journal of Multilingualism*, *18*(2), 183–189.

Kusters, Annelies & Sujit Sahasrabudhe. 2018. Language ideologies on the difference between gesture and sign. *Language & Communication*, *60*, 44–63.

Lackner, Andrea. 2018. *Functions of head and body movements in Austrian Sign Language*. Berlin: Walter de Gruyter.

Lackner, Andrea. 2019. Describing non manuals in sign language. *Grazer Linguistische Studien*, *91*(S), 45–103.

Lakoff, George. 1987. *Women, fire, and dangerous things: What categories reveal about the mind*. Chicago, IL: University of Chicago Press.

Lakoff, George & Mark Johnson. 1980. *Metaphors we live by*. Chicago, IL: University of Chicago Press.

Lakoff, George & Mark Johnson. 1999. *Philosophy in the flesh: The embodied mind and its challenge to western thought*. New York: Basic Books.

Lane, Harlan. 1984. *When the mind hears: A history of the deaf*. New York: Random House.

Lane, Harlan & François Grosjean. 1980. *Recent perspectives on American sign language*. Hillsdale, NJ: Lawrence Erlbaum Associates.

Langacker, Ronald W. 2002. The control cycle: Why grammar is a matter of life and death. *Proceedings of the Annual Meeting of the Japanese Cognitive Linguistics Association*, *2*, 193–220.

Langacker, Ronald W. 2003. Constructions in cognitive grammar. *English Linguistics*, *20*(1), 41–83.

Langacker, Ronald W. 2014. Culture and cognition, lexicon and grammar. In Masataka Yamaguchi, Dennis Tay, & Benjamin Blount (eds.), *Approaches to language, culture, and cognition: The intersection of cognitive linguistics and linguistic anthropology* (pp. 27–49). New York: Palgrave Macmillan.

Langacker, Ronald W. 2019. Levels of reality. *Languages*, *4*(22), 1–20.

Langacker, Ronald W. 1975. Functional stratigraphy. *Chicago Linguistic Society: Parasession on functionalism*, *351*(14), 307–357.

Langacker, Ronald W. 1979. Grammar as image. *Linguistic Notes from La Jolla La Jolla, Cal.*, 87–126.

Langacker, Ronald W. 1987. *Foundations of cognitive grammar: Volume I, Theoretical prerequisites*. Stanford, CA: Stanford University Press.

Langacker, Ronald W. 1991a. *Concept, image, and symbol: The cognitive basis of grammar*. Berlin: Mouton de Gruyter.

Langacker, Ronald W. 1991b. *Foundations of cognitive grammar. Volume II, Descriptive application*. Stanford, CA: Stanford University Press.

Langacker, Ronald W. 1993. Reference-point constructions. *Cognitive Linguistics*, *4*, 1–38.

Langacker, Ronald W. 2000. *Grammar and conceptualization*. Berlin: Mouton de Gruyter.

Langacker, Ronald W. 2008. *Cognitive grammar: A basic introduction*. Oxford: Oxford University Press.

Langacker, Ronald W. 2009. *Investigations in cognitive grammar* (42). Berlin: Walter de Gruyter.

Langacker, Ronald W. 2013. Modals: Striving for control. In Juana I. Marín-Arrese, Marta Carretero, Jorge A. Hita, & Johan Van der Auwera (eds.), *English modality: Core, periphery and evidentiality* (pp. 3–56). Walter de Gruyter.

Langacker, Ronald W. 2016a. Baseline and elaboration. *Cognitive Linguistics*, *27*(3), 405–439.

Langacker, Ronald W. 2016b. *Nominal structure in cognitive grammar*. Lubin: Marie-Curie Skłodowska University Press.

Langacker, Ronald W. 2017. Evidentiality in cognitive grammar. In Juana Isabel Marín-Arrese, Gerda Haßler, & Marta Carretero (eds.), *Evidentiality revisited* (pp. 13–55). Amsterdam: John Benjamins.

Liddell, Scott K. 1990. Four functions of a locus: Reexamining the structure of space in ASL. In Cell Lucas (ed.), *Sign language research: Theoretical issues* (pp. 176–198). Washington, DC: Gallaudet University Press.

Liddell, Scott K. 1995. Real, surrogate, and token space: Grammatical consequences in ASL. In Karen Emmorey & Judy Riley (eds.), *Language, gesture, and space* (pp. 19–41). Hillsdale, NJ: Lawrence Erlbaum Associates.

Liddell, Scott K. 1998. Grounded blends, gestures, and conceptual shifts. *Cognitive Linguistics*, *9*, 283–314.

Liddell, Scott K. 2000a. Blended spaces and deixis in sign language discourse. In David McNeill (ed.), *Language and gesture* (pp. 331–357). Cambridge: Cambridge University Press.

Liddell, Scott K. 2000b. Indicating verbs and pronouns: Pointing away from agreement. In Karen Emmorey & Harlan Lane (eds.), *The signs of language revisited: An anthology to honor Ursula Bellugi and Edward Klima* (pp. 303–320). Mahwah, NJ: Lawrence Erlbaum.

Liddell, Scott K. 2003. *Grammar, gesture, and meaning in American Sign Language*. New York: Cambridge University Press.

Liddell, Scott K. & Robert E. Johnson. 1989. American Sign Language: The phonological base. *Sign Language Studies*, *64*, 195–278.

Liddell, Scott K. & Robert E. Johnson. 2019. Sign language articulators on phonetic bearings. *Sign Language Studies*, *20*(1), 132–172.

Lillo-Martin, Diane & Richard P. Meier. 2011. On the linguistic status of "agreement" in sign languages. *Theoretical Linguistics*, *37*(3/4), 95–141.

Maier, Emar, Kees De Schepper, & Martine Zwets. 2013. The pragmatics of person and imperatives in sign language of the Netherlands. *Research in Language*, *11*(4), 359–376.

Martínez, Rocío & Sherman Wilcox. 2019. Pointing and placing: Nominal grounding in Argentine Sign Language. *Cognitive Linguistics*, *30*(1), 85–121.

Massone, Maria Ignacia & Rocío Anabel Martinez. 2012. Capítulo 7: Morfología de la LSA: Procesos flexionales. In Maria Ignacia Massone & Rocío Anabel Martinez (eds.), *Curso de Lengua de Señas Argentina* (pp. 1–12). Mendoza: Cultura Sorda.

Matlock, Teenie. 2005. Fictive motion as cognitive simulation. *Memory and Cognition*, *32*, 1389–1400.

McKee, Rachel & Sophia Wallingford. 2011. "So, well, whatever": Discourse functions of *palm-up* in New Zealand Sign Language. *Sign Language & Linguistics*, *14*(2), 213–247.

McKenzie, Robert T. 1924. *Exercise in education and medicine* (3rd ed.). Philadelphia, PA: W. B. Saunders.

McNeill, David. 1992. *Hand and mind: What gestures reveal about thought*. Chicago, IL: University of Chicago Press.

McNeill, David. 2000. *Language and gesture*. Cambridge: Cambridge University Press.

Meier, Richard P. & Diane Lillo-Martin. 2013. The points of language. *Humana.Mente Journal of Philosophical Studies*, *24*, 151–176.

Meir, Irit. 2010. Iconicity and metaphor: Constraints on metaphorical extension of iconic forms. *Language: Journal of the Linguistic Society of America*, *86*, 865–896.

Metzger, Melanie. 1995. Constructed dialogue and constructed action in American Sign Language. In Ceil Lucas (ed.), *Sociolinguistics in deaf communities* (pp. 255–271). Washington, DC: Gallaudet University Press.

Neidle, Carol. 2000. SignStream™: A Database Tool for Research on Visual-Gestural Language. Boston, MA: American Sign Language Linguistic Research Project No. 10, Boston University.

Neisser, Ulrich. 1967. *Cognitive psychology*. New York: Appleton-Century-Crofts.

Nespor, Marina & Wendy Sandler. 1999. Prosody in Israeli Sign Language. *Language and Speech*, *42*, 143–176.

Nikolaeva, Irina. 2016. Analyses of the semantics of mood. In Jan Nuyts & J. van der Auwera (eds.), *The Oxford handbook of mood and modality* (pp. 68–85). Oxford: Oxford University Press.

Nilsson, Anna-Lena. 2016. Embodying metaphors: Signed language interpreters at work. *Cognitive Linguistics, 27,* 35–65.

Nuyts, Jan & Johan van der Auwera. 2016. *The Oxford handbook of modality and mood.* Oxford: Oxford University Press.

Okrent, A. 2002. A modality-free notion of gesture and how it can help us with the morpheme vs. gesture question in sign language linguistics (or at least give us some criteria to work with). In Richard Meier, Kearsy Cormier, & David Quinto-Pozos (eds.), *Modality and structure in signed and spoken languages* (pp. 175–198). Cambridge: Cambridge University Press.

Oster, Harriet, Douglas Hegley, & Linda Nagel. 1992. Adult judgments and fine-grained analysis of infant facial expressions: Testing the validity of a priori coding formulas. *Developmental Psychology, 28*(6), 1115–1131.

Özyürek, Asli. 2012. Gesture. In Roland Pfau, Markus Steinbach & Bencie Woll (eds.), *Sign language: An international handbook* (pp. 626–646). Berlin: Mouton. DOI: https://doi.org/10.1515/9783110261325.626.

Padden, Carol. 1986. *Verbs and role-shifting in American Sign Language.* Proceedings from Proceedings of the Fourth National Symposium on Sign Language Research and Teaching.

Pereiro, Carmen Cabeza & Ana Fernández Soneira. 2004. The expression of time in Spanish Sign Language (LSE). *Sign Language & Linguistics, 7*(1), 63–82.

Perniss, Pamela M. 2007. Space and iconicity in German sign language (DGS). *Nijmegen, MPI Series in Psycholinguistics, 45.*

Pfau, Roland & Josep Quer. 2007. On the syntax of negation and modals in Catalan Sign Language and German Sign Language. *Trends in Linguistics Studies and Monographs, 188,* 1–30.

Pfau, Roland & Markus Steinbach. 2011. Grammaticalization in sign languages. In Bernd Heine & Heiko Narrog (eds.), *The Oxford handbook of grammaticalization* (pp. 683–695). Oxford: Oxford University Press. www.oxfordhand books.com/view/10.1093/oxfordhb/9780199586783.001.0001/oxfordhb-9780199586783-e-56.

Port, Robert F. & Adam P. Leary. 2005. Against formal phonology. *Language: Journal of the Linguistic Society of America, 81*(4), 927–964.

Pulleyblank, Edwin G. 1987. Duality of patterning: Responding to Armstrong & Stokoe. *Sign Language Studies, 55,* 175–181.

Pulleyblank, Edwin G. 2011. The meaning of duality of patterning and its importance in language evolution. *Sign Language Studies, 51,* 1–33.

Quer, Josep. 2011. When agreeing to disagree is not enough: Further arguments for the linguistic status of sign language agreement. *Theoretical Linguistics, 37,* 189–196.

Quer, Josep. 2016. Reporting with and without role shift: Sign language strategies of complementation. In Roland Pfau, Markus Steinbach, & Annika Herrmann (eds.), *A matter of complexity: Subordination in Sign Languages* (pp. 204–230). Berlin: De Gruyter Mouton. https://doi.org/10.1515/9781501503238-009/html.

Rovelli, Carlo. 2014. *Reality is not what it seems: The journey to quantum gravity.* New York: Riverhead Books.

Salazar-García, Ventura. 2018. Modality in Spanish Sign Language (LSE) revisited: A functional account. *Open Linguistics, 4*(1), 391–417.

Saltzman, Elliot & J. A. Scott Kelso. 2009. Skilled actions: A task-dynamic approach. *Psychological Review, 94*, 1–48.

Sandler, Wendy. 1999. Prosody in two natural language modalities. *Language and Speech, 42*, 127–142.

Sandler, Wendy. 2009. Symbiotic symbolization by hand and mouth in sign language. *Semiotica: Journal of the International Association for Semiotic Studies/Revue de l'Association Internationale de Sémiotique, 174*, 241–275.

Schembri, Adam, Kearsy Cormier, & Jordan Fenlon. 2018. Indicating verbs as typologically unique constructions: Reconsidering verb "agreement" in sign languages. *Glossa: A Journal of General Linguistics, 3*(1), 1–40.

Schiffrin, Deborah. 1981. Tense variation in narrative. *Language: Journal of the Linguistic Society of America, 57*(1), 45–62.

Schneider, David M. 1976. Notes toward a theory of culture. In Keith Basso & Henry A. Selby (eds.), *Meaning in anthropology* (pp. 197–220). Albuquerque, NM: University of New Mexico Press.

Shaffer, Barbara. 2002. CAN'T: The negation of modal notions in ASL. *Sign Language Studies, 3*, 34–53.

Shaffer, Barbara. 2004. Information ordering and speaker subjectivity: Modality in ASL. *Cognitive Linguistics, 15*(2), 175–195.

Shaffer, Barbara. 2012. Reported speech as an evidentiality strategy in American Sign Language. In Barbara Dancygier & Eve Sweetser (eds.), *Viewpoint in language: A multimodal perspective* (pp. 139–155). Cambridge: Cambridge University Press.

Shaffer, Barbara & Terry Janzen. 2016. Modality and mood in American Sign Language. In Jan Nuyts & Johann van der Auwera (eds.), *The Oxford Handbook of Mood and Modality* (pp. 448–469). Oxford: Oxford University Press.

Shaffer, Barbara, Maria Josep Jarque, & Sherman Wilcox. 2011. The expression of modality: Conversational data from two signed languages. In Márcia Teixeira Nogueira & Maria Fábiola Vasconcelos Lopes (eds.), *Modo e modalidade: gramática, discurso e interação* (pp. 11–39). Fortaleza: Edições UFC.

Shenhav, Amitai, Sebastian Musslick, Falk Lieder, et al. 2017. Toward a rational and mechanistic account of mental effort. *Annual Review of Neuroscience, 40,* 99–124.

Silva, Adelaide Hercília Pescatori & André Nogueira Xavier. 2018. Libras and Articulatory Phonology. *Gradus – Brazilian Journal of Laboratory Phonology, 3*(1), 103–124.

Siyavoshi, Sara. 2019. Hands and faces: The expression of modality in ZEI, Iranian Sign Language. *Cognitive Linguistics, 30*(4), 655–686.

Siyavoshi, Sara & Sherman Wilcox. 2021. Exerting control: The grammatical meaning of facial displays in signed languages. *Cognitive Linguistics, 32*(4), 609–639.

Stokoe, William C. 2005. Sign language structure: An outline of the visual communication systems of the American deaf. 1960. *J Deaf Stud Deaf Educ, 10*(1), 3–37.

Stokoe, William C. 1980a. Review: The Signs of Language by Edward S. Klima and Ursula Bellugi. *Language: Journal of the Linguistic Society of America, 56*(4), 893–899.

Stokoe, William C. 1960. *Sign language structure: An outline of the visual communication systems of the American deaf* (8 Studies in Linguistics Occasional Papers). Buffalo: University of Buffalo.

Stokoe, William C. 1980b. Sign language structure. *Annual Review of Anthropology, 9,* 365–470.

Stokoe, William C. 1991. Semantic phonology. *Sign Language Studies, 71,* 107–114.

Stokoe, William C. 1994. Discovering a neglected language. *Sign Language Studies, 85,* 377–382.

Stokoe, William C., Dorothy Casterline, & Carl Croneberg. 1965. *A dictionary of American Sign Language on linguistic principles.* Washington, DC: Gallaudet College Press.

Stokoe, William C. Jr. 1948. The sources of Sir Launfal: Lanval and Graelent. *PMLA: Publications of the Modern Language Association of America, 63*(2), 392–404.

Stokoe, William C. Jr. 1955. The double problem of *Sir Degaré. PMLA: Publications of the Modern Language Association of America, 70*(3), 518–534.

Streeck, Jürgen. 2009. *Gesturecraft: The manufacture of meaning.* Amsterdam: John Benjamins.

Sturtevant, William C. 1964. Studies in ethnoscience. *American Anthropologist, 66*(3), 99–131.

Talmy, Leonard. 2018. *The targeting system of language.* Cambridge, MA: MIT Press.

Tannen, Deborah. 1986. Introducing constructed dialogue in Greek and American conversational and literary narrative. In Florian Coulmas (ed.), *Direct and indirect speech* (pp. 11–32). Berlin: Mouton de Gruyter Berlin.

Taub, Sarah. 2001. *Language in the body: Iconicity and metaphor in American Sign Language*. Cambridge: Cambridge University Press.

Thelen, Esther & Linda B. Smith. 1994. *A dynamic systems approach to the development of cognition and action*. Cambridge, MA: The MIT Press.

Tyrone, Martha E., Hosung Nam, Elliot Saltzman, Gaurav Mathur, & Louis M. Goldstein. 2010. Prosody and movement in American Sign Language: A task-dynamics approach. *Speech Prosody, 100957*, 1–4.

Van Hoek, Karen. 1997. *Anaphora and conceptual structure*. Chicago, IL: University of Chicago Press.

Walls, Gordon. 1942. *The vertebrate retina and its adaptive radiation*. Bloomfield Hills, MI: Cranbrook Press.

Wilbur, Ronnie B. 1987. *American Sign Language: Linguistic and applied dimensions*. Boston, MA: College-Hill Press.

Wilbur, Ronnie B. 1990. Intonation and focus in American Sign Language. *Proceedings Eastern States Conference on Linguistics (ESCOL), 7*, 320–331.

Wilbur, Ronnie B. 1999. Stress in ASL: Empirical Evidence and Linguistic Issues. *Language and Speech, 42*, 229–250.

Wilbur, Ronnie B. 2013. The point of agreement: Changing how we think about sign language, gesture, and agreement. *Sign language and Linguistics, 16*, 221–258.

Wilcox, Phyllis Perrin. 1996. Deontic and epistemic modals in ASL: A discourse analysis. In Adele E. Goldberg (ed.), *Conceptual structure, discourse, and language* (pp. 481–492). Stanford, CA: Center for the Study of Language and Information.

Wilcox, Phyllis Perrin. 2000. *Metaphor in American Sign Language*. Washington, DC: Gallaudet University Press.

Wilcox, Sherman. 2004. Gesture and language: Cross-linguistic and historical data from signed languages. *Gesture, 4*, 43–75.

Wilcox, Sherman. 2009. Symbol and symptom: Routes from gesture to signed language. *Annual Review of Cognitive Linguistics, 7*, 89–110.

Wilcox, Sherman & Rocío Martínez. 2020. The conceptualization of space: Places in signed language discourse. *Frontiers In Psychology, 11*, 1406.

Wilcox, Sherman & Corrine Occhino. 2016. Constructing signs: Place as a symbolic structure in signed languages. *Cognitive Linguistics, 27*, 371–404.

Wilcox, Sherman, Paolo Rossini, & Elena Antinoro Pizzuto. 2010. Grammaticalization in sign languages. In Diane Brentari (ed.), *Sign languages* (pp. 332–354). Cambridge: Cambridge University Press.

Wilcox, Sherman & Barbara Shaffer. 2006. Modality in American Sign Language. In William Frawley (ed.), *The expression of modality* (pp. 207–237). Berlin: Mouton de Gruyter.

Wilcox, Sherman & Barbara Shaffer. 2017. Evidentiality and information source in signed languages. In Alexandra Y. Aikhenvald (ed.), *Oxford handbook of evidentiality* (pp. 741–754). Oxford: Oxford University Press.

Wilcox, Sherman & Phyllis Wilcox. 2003. Feeling metonymy and metaphor: Evidence from American Sign Language derivational morphology. *International Cognitive Linguistics Association.*

Wilcox, Sherman, Phyllis Wilcox, & Maria Josep Jarque. 2003. Mappings in conceptual space: Metonymy, metaphor, and iconicity in two signed languages. *Jezikoslovlje, 4*(1), 139–156.

Wilcox, Sherman & Phyllis Perrin Wilcox. 1995. The gestural expression of modality in American Sign Language. In Joan Bybee & Suzanne Fleischman (eds.), *Modality in grammar and discourse* (pp. 135–162). Amsterdam: John Benjamins.

Wilcox, Sherman, Rocío Martínez & Diego Morales. 2022. The conceptualization of space in signed languages: Placing the signer in narratives. In Andreas Jucker & Heiko Hausendorf (ed.), *Pragmatics of space* (pp. 63–94). Berlin: De Gruyter Mouton.

Winston, Betsy. 1995. Spatial mapping in comparative discourse frames. In Karen Emmorey & Judy Reilly (eds.), *Language, gesture, and space* (pp. 87–114). Hillsdale, NJ: Lawrence Erlbaum.

Xavier, André Nogueira & Sherman Wilcox. 2014. Necessity and possibility modals in Brazilian Sign Language (Libras). *Linguistic Typology, 18,* 449–488.

Zeshan, Ulrike. 2004. Interrogative constructions in signed languages: Crosslinguistic perspectives. *Language: Journal of the Linguistic Society of America, 80*(1), 7–39.

Cambridge Elements ☰

Cognitive Linguistics

Sarah Duffy
Northumbria University

Sarah Duffy is Senior Lecturer in English Language and Linguistics at Northumbria University. She has published primarily on metaphor interpretation and understanding, and her forthcoming monograph for Cambridge University Press (co-authored with Michele Feist) explores *Time, Metaphor, and Language* from a cognitive science perspective. Sarah is Review Editor of the journal, *Language and Cognition*, and Vice President of the UK Cognitive Linguistics Association.

Nick Riches
Newcastle University

Nick Riches is a Senior Lecturer in Speech and Language Pathology at Newcastle University. His work has investigated language and cognitive processes in children and adolescents with autism and developmental language disorders, and he is particularly interested in usage-based accounts of these populations.

About the Series

Cambridge Elements in Cognitive Linguistics aims to extend the theoretical and methodological boundaries of cognitive linguistics. It will advance and develop established areas of research in the discipline, as well as address areas where it has not traditionally been explored and areas where it has yet to become well-established.

Cambridge Elements ≡

Cognitive Linguistics

9 781009 486842